20/20 VISION

20/20 VISION

SEEING GOD CLEARLY

BY BOBBY MURPHY

XULON PRESS

Xulon Press
2301 Lucien Way #415
Maitland, FL 32751
407.339.4217
www.xulonpress.com

Printed in the United States of America.

ISBN-13: 9781545622353

TABLE OF CONTENTS

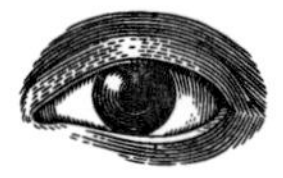

INTRODUCTION

"Captivate people with a vision of God." One night, I was deliberating over what God wanted me to do with the rest of my life, however long that might be. I was alone with Him in solitude and silence and as I was, He spoke to me through the still small voice of the Holy Spirit those very words.

My overriding concern at this juncture of my life is that people will highly esteem the living God and it grieves me that they don't. I find myself growing increasingly sensitive, for instance, to our culture's chronic and almost obsessive use of the God-demeaning expression, "Oh my God" or "OMG". It's grating to me because I hold Him in the highest possible regard and it's paramount to me that others will do the same.

That's why I should have known what God wants me to do. A basic principle of divine guidance is that we can determine what God is calling us to do for Him by determining what we want most to do for Him. What I want most to do for Him is to assist others in adoring Him. I can, therefore, confidently conclude that's what He's calling me to do, which the Holy Spirit's still small voice that night confirmed.

The writing of this book, *20/20 Vision*, represents my best efforts to answer His call. Adoring God isn't a response that we can conjure up by gritting our teeth and willing it. It's a natural response instead that flows gently and gradually from understanding and experiencing His absolute and unqualified goodness and greatness. As our "head-knowledge" and experiential knowledge of Him together grow so does our adoration of Him. My express purpose for writing *20/20 Vision* is to teach the head-knowledge that underlies the experiential knowledge that cultivates and sustains adoration of God.

I've borrowed the word "Vision" from one of Christendom's most notable and influential hymns that happens to be my favorite, "Be Thou My Vision." Typical of medieval Irish poetry, its lyrics draw on traditional Irish culture and employ heroic imagery such as "High King of Heaven" to portray the greatness of God. His greatness is the ground of the common sense desire expressed in the hymn's first stanza:

Be Thou my vision, oh Lord of my heart
Naught be all else to me, save that Thou art
Thou my best thought by day or by night
Waking or sleeping, Thy presence my light.[1]

Note the yearning here to make God our "vision." I mentioned head-knowledge of God and the word "vision" is synonymous with that. It refers to how we see or perceive Him and as the first stanza implies, our aim in life should be to have a 20/20 vision of Him. It should be to see Him clearly, as He is in all of His infinite and perfect goodness and greatness.

It should be not only because it's the basis of adoring Him but also because of the part it plays in our worldview. Our worldview is the beliefs we have about the matters that we must and want to deal with on a day-to-day basis such as money, politics, sex, looks, health, marriage, friendship, work, sports, and countless more. Those beliefs involve a readiness to act as if what is believed is so, making them arbiters of our behavioral lives. A person who runs six miles a day, for example, does so because of what he believes about appearance and/or health. Our worldviews and the beliefs that comprise them do largely direct our practical lives.

There are a host of worldview questions the answers to which constitute our beliefs. The first two of those, "first" as in significance and thus order, are "Does God exist?" and second if so, "What is He like?" Those questions are first and second sequentially because our answers to them condition our answers to all the other worldview questions whatever the subject matter is they address. Suppose we're counseling our teenage son, a high school football player, about the competitive spirit and the part it plays in his performance. If we were to logically trace the advice we give backwards to where it starts, we'd discover it starts with our answers to the first two worldview questions. What we believe about God's existence, the first question, and His nature, the second question, is the bedrock of all our other beliefs and the actions to which they lead.

Our vision of God goes to the second of those questions and is in that sense what I call "the first button" of human life. I'm referencing the guiding rule for buttoning shirts that our mothers or fathers taught us when we were children. You know how it goes: "Get the first button right and you can get the rest of the buttons right. Get the first one wrong and you will get the rest wrong." Metaphorically speaking, our vision of God is the first button. Because our universe and life in it are rooted in His being, if we get our vision of Him right, we *can* get our lives right as well. If we get it wrong, we *will* get our lives wrong as well. It drives and runs our lives more than anything else about us does.

That you're reading this book suggests that you're a functional person who desires in his or her heart of hearts to adore God and to live well. My humble prayer is that this book will assist you in taking the first step in fulfilling those desires of yours, developing a 20/20 vision of God that sees Him clearly. It isn't a baby step you're taking in doing so but a leap really that will open up whole new vistas of God's glorious goodness and greatness to you and in the process a positive newness of adoration of Him and of life itself as well. Enjoy the journey!

DEDICATION

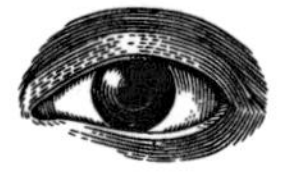

To my wife Jill,
for whom my love is
"the very flame of Yahweh".
(Song of Solomon 8:6)

CHAPTER 1

"HE'S NUMBER '1'"

What is your favorite number? According to assorted informal surveys, most people have a favorite with "7" consistently being the most popular of those and my favorite, "1", consistently being a least popular of those. Most people choose their favorite number based on some personal experience, activity, or event that they associate with it but I chose mine based on the nature of the number itself. "1" may not be the most popular of numbers but it's singularly unique.

Let's test your mathematical skills with a question. Which is greater? Is it the difference between "1" and "2" or between "2" and "1000?" As Quaker author Elton Trueblood pointed out in his book *Foundations for Reconstruction*, it's the difference between "1" and "2".[2] It is because "1" is utterly unique. When we move from "2" to "1000," the difference is enormous mathematically but there is no difference metaphysically. "2" and "1000" are of the same "kind," both being plural. In contrast, when we move from "1" to "2", the difference is slight mathematically but enormous metaphysically. "1" is of an entirely different kind than "1000" and all other numbers. It's singular and they're plural.

This inimitable nature of the number "1" makes it an ideal metaphor for God. He's number "1". As the number "1" is to all other numbers so God is to all other realities.

He Himself reveals this fundamental fact about Him in what is arguably the most remarkable revelation of Scripture. He chose a personal name for Himself and disclosed it to Moses in Exodus 3:14. In the Old Testament world, a name was synonymous with the nature or character of the person who bore it. Hence, when God revealed His personal name, He revealed what is basic about Him. That name in the Hebrew language is *Yahweh*, which according to Exodus 3:14 means "I am who I am" or in its shortened form "I am."

What Reality Is

The Hebrew word *Yahweh* derives from the verb "to be." It connotes "what is." It's about reality in other words. Reality has two nuances. First, it's what objectively exists. *Objectively* means that it exists even if we don't know or believe it does. Second, reality is also what is true or so. Everything that exists, whether it's animate or inanimate, has its own peculiar nature or order that characterizes it. It "is as it is" so to speak. *What is true or so* refers to what the nature or order of things naturally causes to happen or occur.

Gasoline illustrates the two nuances of reality. First, it objectively exists in tangible form. We can see, feel, taste, and smell it. Second, something is true or so because of its peculiar nature or order. It's an aliphatic hydrocarbon made up of molecules composed of nothing but hydrogen and carbon atoms arranged in particular chains. This nature or order makes its fumes highly flammable. As a result, if a lit ash from a cigarette unites with gasoline vapors, they'll explode and burn.

Gasoline with its highly flammable vapors is the very embodiment of reality. Reality is what exists and what is true or so because of the nature or order of what exists.

Acting Contrary to the Nature of Reality

Reality of course is vital to us all. The very substance of our day-to-day lives consists of acting upon it and experiencing the natural consequences of how we do so. We have casual sex with someone, give good for evil, max out our credit cards, raise our children with or without discipline, and text while we drive. In each of those actions and choices and countless more, we're acting upon reality and experiencing the spiritual, psychological, physiological, relational, financial, and circumstantial consequences of doing so. Whether we're conscious of it or not, that is the essence of our day-to-day lives. Grasp what that means. How we act upon reality in a particular circumstance determines how poorly or well things go for us in it.

You and I have two options in that regard.

One is to spit into the wind. Singer-song writer Jim Croce released a song in 1972 about a tough guy named Jim, titled appropriately *You Don't Mess Around with Jim*. The song's refrain goes like this:

You don't tug on Superman's cape
You don't spit into the wind
You don't pull the mask off the old Long Ranger
And you don't mess around with Jim.[3]

Croce used an idiom to which we can all relate, "Spit *into* the wind." The idea is that we act contrary to reality. Let's go back to gasoline again. Someone posted a picture of a woman pumping gasoline into a container with a lit cigarette in the fingers of the hand holding the container. Reflecting on the nature of gasoline, she was acting contrary to it. She was spitting into the wind and from time to time, so do we. We think, feel, will, act, or react inconsistently with the nature or order of things that exist.

As Croce's refrain so colorfully depicts it, things go poorly when we do. We all know by hard experience what happens when we spit into the wind. Something disgusting happens. Others and we get wet. Spitting *into* the wind is a mini-parable. It teaches us something about acting inconsistently with the nature or order of things. In one way or another and to one extent or another, it's always detrimental to others and/or us when we do.

Take something as workaday as a person engaging us in conversation. Let's think about the nature of humans in that context. What people say comes from inside them. It comes from their minds – from their mental and emotional processes – so that they highly value what they say and want others to do the same. But suppose that we spit *into* the wind by not valuing what they say. We're consistently "me-deep" in conversation and dominate it. What is true or so is that people will dislike and avoid us if we do.

Anyone who dominates conversation has chosen the first option that is before us in every circumstance of day-to-day life. We spit *into* the wind. We act contrary to reality. It always harms others and/or us when we do.

Acting According to the Nature of Reality

There's a second option before us. We spit *with* the wind. We act according to reality in other words. We act consistently with the nature or order of things that exist.

Things go well in the particular circumstance before us when we do. Let's go back to someone engaging us in conversation. Suppose that we spit *with* the wind. We act according to the nature of humans. Knowing that they highly value what they say, we do the same and listen attentively as they speak. We "hang on their every word" as we say it, appropriately commenting and asking questions in response. An old aphorism articulates what is true or so as a result. A good listener is a silent flatterer. Intently listening flatters people. It uplifts their spirits and endears them to us.

This relational response exemplifies the second option before us. Spit with the wind. Act according to reality. In one way or another and to one extent or another, it's always beneficial to others and/or us when we do.

Former Calvin Seminary President Cornelius Platinga sums up the two options before us with these insightful words: "Wisdom in Scripture is, broadly speaking, the knowledge of God's world and the knack of fitting oneself into it. To be wise is to know reality and then accommodate yourself to it. Folly is a stubborn swimming against the stream of the universe . . . spitting into the wind . . . coloring outside the lines."[4] The terminology he uses is enlightening. To act according to reality is to *accommodate it*. It's to *fit ourselves into it*. Life goes poorly for others and/or us when we don't. It goes well when we do. It really is as simple as that.

God as the Foundation of Reality

That train of thought leads us back to where we began, Exodus 3:14 and God. This verse is *the* fundamental of all revelations about Him. By taking the verb form "to be" as His name and using it to describe the essence of His being, He was declaring that He is the foundation of all reality, the ground of all being, and He is!

Remember the metaphor with which we began. God is number 1. As the number "1" is to all other numbers so He is to all other realities, both spiritual (non-material) and material. Simply put, He is in the substance of His being an utterly separate kind of reality. He is totally different than anyone or anything else that exists.

Notice I said "different than" not "above." He is not just *above* or *the highest of* all reality. He is not just *eminent* or *pre-eminent*. Those words incorrectly imply that He is like other realities in His substance but just superior. That isn't so. He is as different in nature than anyone or anything else that exists as the number 1 is different in nature than any other numbers. Bill and Gloria Gaither wrote a song years ago titled *You're Something Special*. It claims about each person that "You're the only one of your kind."[5] It's an inspirational thought but untrue. That cannot be said of any person because all of us are of the same "kind." All of us are humans. It can be said though of God. In relation to all other reality, He's the only one of His kind. As we'll learn in detail in later chapters, no one else and nothing else are even remotely like Him. He's an utterly separate kind of reality.

An analogy helps explain it. Think of a pre-eminent kind of reality like the archangel Michael. He has powers of consciousness and activity and a loveliness of character that almost defy description. Also think of a banal kind of reality like a slug in your garden. The slug is as elementary a form of life as Michael is pre-eminent. It has only minimal powers of consciousness and activity and no character or personality in even the slightest measure. It doesn't take a rocket scientist to figure it out. The difference between the nature of Michael on the one hand and the nature of a slug on the other is almost immeasurable. But as great as that is, the difference between God and Michael is greater. God is more different in nature than Michael than Michael is different in nature than a slug. Michael is more like the slug in other words than He is like God. That's because he isn't like God, at all. And neither is anyone or anything else.

Anyone else includes Satan. *Yahoo! Answers* posted the following question, "Are God and the Devil equal opposites?"[6] The answer is "No." The devil is more like the slug in your garden than He is like God because he isn't like God in kind at all. The words "equal" and "opposite" have no application to God because as the psalmist rightly declares in Psalm 86:10, "You *alone* are God." He is the only one of His kind who has no equals or opposites.

That means it isn't exaggerating to say that God is the very foundation of all reality; that He is the very ground of all being. Or to say it another way, He is *ultimate reality*.

Acting According to the Nature of God

Because He is, it's imperative that we act according to the nature of His being. The "nature of His being" refers to what we call His attributes, a selection of which Chapters 3 through 18 identify and explain. We must habitually accommodate or fit ourselves into those attributes. The overall quality of our one life on earth depends on it.

Every sane person on earth desires and pursues the same quality of life. The immigrant laborer and the Wall Street Banker have this in common. Each craves and seeks an ongoing and consistent experience of the foundational fruit of the Holy Spirit – love, joy, and peace (Galatians 5:22). The Bible fleshes out what this looks like in the real world of day-to-day life: always having to get our own way no longer burdens us; we're glad not sad when others eclipse us; we're contented with little or much; we welcome criticism, not resent and reject it; we enjoy simple things more than others enjoy extravagant things; we stand strong and hopeful in the storms of life; and much more. Love, joy, and peace, in other words, primarily characterize our inner and outer lives. Jesus referred to this as abundance of life in John 10:10, assuming in doing so that it's the deepest longing of humans.

He was right. It is. All of us want abundance of life and the good news is that we can have it, if we live pursuant to the nature of God. Make it our common practice to think, feel, will, act, and react consistently with His attributes as I explain them in Chapters 3 through 18. We'll live abundantly if we do. Love, joy, and peace will unceasingly abound inside us and out. Why? It's because He's the foundation of all reality. He's number "1."

CHAPTER 2

"20/20 VISION"

How is your vision? According to the Vision Council of America, approximately 30% of Americans are near-sighted and 60% are far-sighted. Because they are, 75% of adults wear either eyeglasses or contact lenses, reflecting their desire to have 20/20 vision. All of us want to see the material world around us as clearly as we can and with corrective lenses, most of us do.

But how well do we see the spiritual or non-material world around us, including its most glorious inhabitant, God? Do we see Him clearly, as He is? If we don't, we must because doing so is the very first and most basic step we take in acting according to His nature. After all, we can't act according to His nature unless we know what it is. So, let's know what it is by making our vision of Him 20/20, an aim we can achieve by learning and living out the Second of the Ten Commandments.

The Second Commandment, recorded in Deuteronomy 5:8-10, charges us in verse 8, "You shall not make for yourself any graven image, or any likeness of what is in heaven above or on the earth beneath or in the water under the earth." Deuteronomy 4:15-18 is a little commentary on this commandment, verse 16 stating it a bit differently, "Do not act corruptly and make a graven image in the form of any figure."

The Second Commandment - the Letter of the Law

Let's determine the *letter of the law* of this commandment.

The Hebrew word translated "graven image" or "idol" in some versions connotes something that is chiseled or carved. In the ancient world, that something was wood, stone, or cast metal such as silver or gold. Most images were made of wood because it was easiest to form.

The Hebrew words translated "likeness" and "figure" mean that the wood, stone, or metal was chiseled or carved to look like something that's real. According to the language in the texts, that something real is birds, fish, water mammals, animals, or even humans.

Deuteronomy 5:9 discloses the action that the Commandment prohibits. It's to "worship" or "serve" what the images represent, which raises an issue. What do they represent? The answer is that they represent the one true God, Yahweh. The Second Commandment isn't about making images that represent false gods and goddesses. The First Commandment implicitly prohibits that. What it is about is making images that represent Yahweh, as the Israelites did in Exodus 32. They worshipped Him while Moses was on Mount Sinai by worshipping a golden calf that represented Him. He, in the Second Commandment, forbids making that image or any image that represents Him.

He explains why He forbids it in Deuteronomy 4:15. It's because He doesn't have "any form" to quote Him in that verse. Jesus said it differently in John 4:24 but the meaning is the same, "God is spirit." As we'll learn in Chapter 3, He doesn't have material substance. He isn't made up of atoms and molecules and doesn't have a brain or body. But images by their very nature have form and in having it convey something about Him that isn't so, that He's material not spiritual. They also convey that He's localized – that He's only present where the image is. But as we'll learn in Chapter 7, He isn't. He's omnipresent instead, that is, everywhere present with His entire being at the same time.

We now know the *letter of the law* regarding the Second Commandment. Don't worship God by worshipping images that represent Him because they convey ideas about Him that aren't so.

The Second Commandment - the Spirit of the Law

But so what? Let's face it. None of us are going to make images that represent God and worship them any time soon. So how does the Second Commandment apply to us? There is a *spirit of the law* here and it's this. Envision (think about) God as He is. If we envision Him as He is, we're keeping the Second Commandment. If we envision Him as He is not, we're breaking it.

This spirit of the law evokes a provocative personal question that we need to ask and answer. Am I keeping or breaking the Second Commandment? In his classic book *The Knowledge of the Holy*, A.W. Tozer postulated that most Christians, if they were honest, would have to answer it in the negative. He wrote as follows: "It is my opinion that the Christian conception of God current in these middle years of the twentieth century is so decadent as to be utterly beneath the dignity of the Most High God and actually to constitute for professed believers something amounting to a moral calamity."[7] He penned those words 60 years ago, but they're as applicable today as they were then. The vision of God that resides in the minds of many if not most professing Christians is beneath Him. It doesn't do justice to the magnificence of His being and breaks the spirit of the Second Commandment.

Professing Christians can and do break the spirit of the Second Commandment in one or both of two ways.

First, some envision God as *other* than He is. Four centuries ago, Blasé Pascal declared that God created man in His own image and that man then returned the favor. Many people do make God in their own image, perceiving Him not as He is but as they want Him to be. They choose to believe things about Him that justify what they value, desire, and do. That choice of theirs makes their vision of Him, to one degree or another, an inaccurate one.

The prosperity gospel is perhaps the most striking example of this in our own cultural context. Professing Christians value and pursue extravagance and create a God in their minds who endorses them doing so. They perceive Him to be a sort of indulgent father figure who loves lavishing luxurious gifts upon His children. That perception of theirs then validates the materialistic way in which they themselves are living.

Professing Christians can and do make a second mistake. The first is envisioning God as *other* than He is – believing things about Him that aren't so. The second is envisioning Him as *less* than He is – not knowing and believing things about Him that are so. Their vision of Him, in other words, is incomplete. They don't know about Him what they should and could know if they intended it.

First, they don't know some or even most of His revealed attributes. After commenting to a long-established Christian that God is the most joyful being in the universe, she replied, "I never heard that before." Or after mentioning that God is immutable to another, he replied the same. Suppose I asked you to list every attribute of God that you've identified. How many would be on your list? Five? Ten? Twenty? What revealed attributes of His have you identified? What revealed attributes of His have you not identified? If you're like many if not most Christians, the ones you have not identified outnumber the ones you have.

Many Christians' vision of God can also be incomplete because they know little or nothing about the attributes they've identified. You probably know, for instance, that God is omniscient or all-knowing. But how much do you know about that? Suppose I asked you to write all the details about His omniscience that you know. How much would you be able to write? If you're a typical Christian, it's very little. Most

Christians know only generally not particularly about the attributes they've identified.

Those then are the two ways that Christians can and do break the spirit of the Second Commandment. They perceive Him as *other* than He is and/or as *less* than He is. Their vision of Him is *inaccurate* and/or *incomplete*.

Knowing what it means to break the spirit of the Second Commandment assists us by way of contrast to know what it means to keep it. We perceive God *only* as He is. Our vision of Him is *accurate*. We also perceive Him as *much* as He is. Our vision of Him is complete, as complete as it can be at least.

How We Keep the Second Commandment

Now that we know the "what" of keeping the Second Commandment, let's examine the "how." How do we keep it? It's by developing a deliberate and comprehensive vision of God.

When I say "deliberate," I mean as opposed to the "random" way most of us have built our vision of Him. We picked up the ideas about Him that comprise it here and there and in bits and pieces over the years from a variety of sources. We didn't contemplate what we heard or read. We just accepted it and added it to our mishmash of ideas about Him.

The problem is that randomly formed visions of God are always to one degree or another inaccurate and incomplete. The idea that the Trinity is like an egg with its yolk, white, and shell is a case in point. It's so frequently taught that Christians unthinkingly incorporate it into their vision of Him, mistakenly concluding from it that the Father, Son, and Holy Spirit are three separate beings who can and do act apart from each other. Unintentional and haphazard visions of God always see Him as other and less than He is.

It's essential that we make our vision of Him deliberate. We make the decision to see Him as accurately and completely as we can. We then do whatever is necessary to carry out our decision. We incorporate the ideas that comprise our vision of Him purposefully and thoughtfully. A vision of Him developed this way sees Him as He is.

But the vision of Him that we build isn't just deliberate. It's also comprehensive or thorough.

Let's take just a moment at this juncture and lay to rest a mind-bending question, "How many attributes does God have?" A Frederick Faber hymn speaks of the "God of a thousand attributes" but that understates the reality of His being. He has far more than we can even envisage, some of which He's revealed to us. Comprehensive suggests that our vision of Him incorporates most if not all of the ones He's revealed.

But "comprehensive" means more than thorough. It means "specific" as well. Each attribute of God is rich in implications. "Specific" suggests that our vision of Him incorporates the most consequential of those. It descends beyond the surface of general definition into the depths of detail. This specificity in conjunction with thoroughness makes our vision comprehensive.

Now, the comprehensiveness of our vision of God is no small thing. The degree to which our vision shapes us and guides the course of our lives is in direct proportion to the degree that it's comprehensive. The more comprehensive we make it, the more power it has to inspire and manage our persons and lives. Making it that is a two-step process.

The first step is to identify as many of God's attributes as we can. Creation (Romans 1:19-20) and more importantly the Bible reveal those that God wants us to know and that we need to know.

Creation reveals those implicitly so that we know them by drawing inferences from our natural world. We can infer from the complexity of DNA strands, for instance, that God has a prodigious mind.

The Bible reveals attributes explicitly so that we know them by reading it with focus and concentration. What I do is this. Whenever I come across a verse or text in my devotional Bible reading that reveals something about God's nature, I write down what it reveals. So, I read Romans 2:4 in which Paul mentions "the kindness and tolerance and patience of God." I then put all three – kind, tolerant, and patient – on my list of attributes. Or I read James 1:7. God is "the Father of lights, with whom there is no variation or shifting shadow." I then put immutable or unchanging on my list. You get the idea. In the course of our normal Bible reading, we write down every attribute of God that a verse or text reveals. It's a primary means of building a comprehensive vision of Him, one that encompasses most if not all of His revealed attributes.

There's a second step in making our vision of God comprehensive. We dig into the details of each attribute we've identified. We do this deductively. First, we define what the attribute means. Second, we apply the logical relations of implication and contradiction to the definition and draw as many valid conclusions from it as we can. We ask and answer the question, "If this definition is true, what must also be true?" Our answers to that question are the details into which we've dug.

Let me illustrate the two steps for making our vision of God comprehensive. First, I learned from my Bible reading that God is omnipresent. Second, I then descended into the details of His omnipresence. I defined what that attribute of His means. He is everywhere present at the same time with His entire being. Having done so, I applied the logical relations of implication and contradiction to the definition and drew as many valid conclusions from it as I could. One of those is that motion words such as "go," "come," and "arrive" don't apply to God because He's always everywhere there is to go, come, or arrive. A popular billboard presents God saying to humans on earth, "Don't make me come down there," but it's incorrect. He never has to "come down" to earth because He's always here, that is, everywhere on it and in it that it's possible to be. There is never anywhere on it and in it that He isn't fully present.

As you might expect, the two steps for building a comprehensive vision of God, identifying as many of His revealed attributes as we can and digging into the details of each, is something that takes effort. But at the same time, it's something that all of us can do. We don't need any special education or training; just the desire and purposefulness to do it. There is help, however, that's available to us. It's people in the know who have pursued knowing God's attributes through and through. They've identified His revealed attributes and dug into their details. So, we read what they wrote. A.W. Tozer's classic book *The Knowledge of the Holy*, J.I. Packer's book *Knowing God*, and Arthur Pink's book *The Attributes of God* are cases in point.

I certainly don't put myself in the company of these storied authors but *20/20 Vision* is my attempt to assist you in your efforts to build your vision of God. Chapters 3 through 18 identify revealed attributes of God and dig into their details. Notice that each chapter contains three pericopes or sections of thought: the attribute revealed, the attribute explained, and the attribute applied. I've given the last of those, the attribute applied, an emphasis that articles and books about God's attributes usually don't. My purpose in doing so is that our vision of God will not only educate our minds but transform our persons and lives as well, leading to the abundance of life we seek.

I encourage you to read on for what I pray will be the most rewarding pursuit you've ever undertaken – developing a 20/20 vision of God.

CHAPTER 3

"NO BRAIN OR BODY"

God Is Spirit

We start with the attribute of God that is the easiest to identify but perhaps the most difficult to comprehend and accept. He is spirit.

God Is Spirit Revealed

Our own routine experience with God verifies that He is spirit and so does the Bible.

In Exodus 19, God manifested His presence on Mount Sinai by engulfing it with smoke and fire and by causing it to quake. He then spoke to the Israelites the contents of Exodus 20-23. Deuteronomy 4:12, 15 shares the penetrating insight about that encounter of theirs with Him that they "saw no form."

In 4:12 of his first letter, the beloved disciple John similarly notes that "No one has seen God at any time." The Israelites didn't see Him at Mt. Sinai and according to John, no one ever has.

Jesus explains why in John 4:24. He informed the Samaritan woman at the well in one of His most widely known sayings that "God is spirit" (John 4:24). The word "spirit" is an antipode to the word "matter" and makes clear to us that God is not matter.

God Is Spirit Explained

Every "thing" that exists in our material universe has form. Form refers to its structure, which is determined by the arrangement of atoms and molecules that make it up. It's this form of any "thing" that enables us to see it. Light, as we learned in our high school science classes, reflects off its structure and into our eyes.

It's a simple factoid that introduces and clarifies the texts we just examined and our first attribute of God. The reason God can't be seen isn't because He's hiding from us and won't let us see Him. It's because He has no form, no material structure off of which light can reflect and make Him visible to us. Simply put, He isn't made up of atoms and molecules as every "thing" in our material universe is, including us. Or as Jesus said it, He is spirit!

Let's think about us for a moment, by which I mean humans. The First Law of Thermodynamics says that matter can be neither created nor destroyed. That necessarily means that all the atoms that are our bodies were created in Genesis 1:1 making each of us a whole lot older than we think we are. Anyway, every "thing" in the material universe, including you and me, is comprised of atoms and molecules.

But God is not. He is the opposite of what we are. We are matter. He is spirit. He isn't made up of atoms and molecules and unlike us, He has no body and brain and doesn't miss them. [8] I know how off the wall that may sound to you and you're not alone. Because it's all we've ever experienced, many of us hold that consciousness requires a perceptual apparatus and neural processing, a brain in other words, and that activity requires an animating apparatus, a body. They don't. As curious as it may seem to some of us, God has the highest possible levels of consciousness and activity without a body and brain.

But if He is spiritual in that sense, why does the Bible speak of Him as if He has body parts? Verses such as Exodus 33:20, Exodus 3:20, Deuteronomy 33:27, Proverbs 15:3, and Isaiah 59:1 mention the face, hand, arms, eyes, and ear of God. If God isn't bodily, why do these verses speak as if He is?

The answer is a simple one. It's to enable and to enhance understanding. Since we've never experienced consciousness without a brain and activity without a body, we have no literal reference point for comprehending it. Because we don't, God must use figurative language to explain it and that's what He does. We call this figurative language *anthropomorphism*. Anthropomorphisms are descriptions of God's powers and activities in terms of body parts or movements. Like all figures of speech, they aren't to be taken literally. As I've already noted, He doesn't have any body parts including a brain.

Nonetheless, He is in His non-material condition or state able to *act upon* the material universe. In the text to which I referred earlier, for instance, He spoke audibly to the Israelites at Mt. Sinai. He doesn't have a larynx, tongue, or mouth, but can cause vibrations in the air that enter human ears as sound. He's also able to *receive from* the material universe. When we perceive an object like the face a loved one, for instance, we don't see the face itself, just the light that the face reflects. He doesn't have eyes and doesn't need them. He actually perceives, in whatever way it is that He does, the face itself. God's spiritual nature doesn't preclude Him from interacting with matter. On the contrary, he can and does interact with it far more directly and effectively than we can know.

God Is Spirit Applied

Some of God's attributes are more difficult for us to wrap our minds around than others are and God as spirit is one of those. I've concluded from 37 years of pastoral experience that Christians not only struggle conceptually with this particular attribute of His but volitionally as well. The problem isn't just that they can't envision God this way; it's that they don't want to. In their minds, this attribute makes Him less vivid and real and diminishes their ability to interact with Him.

A father's little daughter called out to him from her bedroom that she was afraid to sleep alone. He in turn exhorted her not to be afraid because God was with her. To which she immediately replied, "But I want someone with a face."

Many Christians seem to want what that little girl wanted. They want a God with a face, that is, a material and bodily God. One of their unspoken assumptions is that such a God would be more engaging and engageable than a spiritual One. They would be able to act upon Him and be acted upon by Him more personally if He was material.

I'll never forget explaining God's spiritual nature to a Christian who, annoyed by what I said, responded, "It makes Him less real to me and I don't believe it." Her comment betrays the misguided thinking of many Christians. It's misguided because in reality our interactions with God are more personal and deep not less because He's spirit and not matter.

Consider the lodestar of Biblical promises in John 14:23, "If anyone loves Me, he will keep My word; and My Father will love him, and We will come to him and make Our abode with him." God will be with and in us, Jesus says here. Notice the prepositions I used there, "with" and "in" us. God promises to be a constant presence with and in us if we love Him and do what He says.

No one with a body could keep that promise. The limitations that bodies impose are obvious. First, no humans, including our spouses, can ever be a constant presence *with* us. Their material nature makes them localized so that their bodies could not be always present where we are. Second, no humans can ever be a constant presence *in* us. Their material nature renders them incapable of knowing or even touching us in the very core of our being. My wife, for instance, can never know or touch me in my essence and I can never know or touch her in hers.

But God, just because He's spirit, can do both of those things. Because He's spirit, it's possible for Him to be omnipresent or always *with* us and He is. It's also possible for Him to penetrate into and intertwine Himself with the very fabric of our being and He does. He's able to inhabit and work in our mental, emotional, volitional, and bodily processes as He promises in John 14:23.

The consequence is that we can have an ongoing interactive relationship with Him that's as vivid and real, but more meaningful and deep, than any that we have with humans. Hear that again. It's worth repeating. We can have an ongoing interactive relationship with Him that's as vivid and real, but more meaningful and deep, than any that we have with humans. That He's spirit makes Him not less knowable but more. Our relationship with Him can be a uniquely intimate one in which mind touches mind and heart touches heart.

That means if we don't have a fulfilling relationship with God, the problem isn't with Him and His spiritual nature. The problem is with us that we, being material, haven't learned how to act upon, interact with, and receive the spiritual. But we can learn how. There are certain central activities for engaging the spiritual God who is always with and in us. They include solitude and silence, fasting, study, prayer, lectio divina, practicing the presence, purposeful obedience, the musing of the mind upon Him, worship, thanksgiving, fellowship with His people, and conversation with Him. Learn how to carry out those central practices of life with God. Then carry them out with the consistency and intensity that His utter loveliness and competence dictate that we should. We'll know experientially if we do that in His presence is fullness of joy (Psalm 16:11). That He is spirit and not matter makes it so.

CHAPTER 4

"NOT MADE"

God Is Self-existent

That God is spirit makes possible a second attribute of His, one that alone sets Him apart from all other realities, spiritual and material. He is self-existent.

Self-existence Revealed

In Exodus 3:1-12, God revealed Himself to Moses in a theophany, a visible manifestation of His presence. The theophany in this incidence was a burning bush. Fire needs something outside itself to fuel it or it goes out. That something else can be and sometimes is a bush. But the fire engulfing the bush that Moses saw was unique. You and I have never seen anything like it. According to verse 2, the bush wasn't being consumed, which implies that the fire that enveloped it needed nothing outside itself, including the bush, to burn. The burning bush was a symbolic phenomenon. The fire represented God and it needing nothing outside itself to burn represented that God needs nothing outside Himself to exist.

He further disclosed this aspect of His being to Moses in Exodus 3:13-15. He chose a Hebrew word to be His personal name and a vehicle for His people to understand and remember His quintessence. That word, as we learned in Chapter 1, was *Yahweh*, the meaning of which is either "I am who I am" or "I will be who I will be." God chose that name because of what it connotes. It's that He has always been, is, and always will be.

A New Testament text, Acts 17:25, supplements what the burning bush and the name He chose divulge about God. Attempting to describe what God is like to a group of Greek philosophers, Paul explained one of His attributes this way: "Nor is He served by human hands, as though He needed anything, since He Himself gives to all people life and breath and all things." Notice the two bold assertions that Paul puts forward here. One is that all people and all things are utterly dependent on God to live or exist. The other is that He, in stark contrast, is dependent on nothing to live and exist.

Self-existence Explained

Exodus 3:1-12; Exodus 3:13-15; and Acts 17:25 together reveal an attribute of God that distances Him ontologically from everything else that exists as much if not more so than any other attribute does. He's self-existent.

One of the questions I've been asked most over the years is "Where did God come from?" or its equivalent "Who made God?" An 80 year-old once asked me the same question in the afternoon that a 9 year-old had asked me that morning, "Where did God come from?" People ask that question because of an assumption under which they operate. It's that something, whether it's an object or event, doesn't come from nothing. Every something has a cause. Since God is a something, the reasoning goes, He has a cause. He must have been made.

But He wasn't. He's an ultimate personal being who has the power of being within Himself. He has the possession of life, with the consciousness and the power to act, within Himself. His own existence and life depend upon nothing other than Himself. He needs nothing outside Himself to exist and live. Because He doesn't, it necessarily follows that He has no origin or cause. He didn't come from anywhere. He wasn't made. Simply put, He's self-existent.

The self-existence of God addresses an issue that quantum physicists, cosmologists, and laymen like many of us wrestle with even today. What is the origin of the universe? Where did it come from? Who made it? God's self-existence tells us. An uncaused cause did.

Inquirers into the nature of our universe embrace the principle of causal closure. It states, in its weakest form, that every physical object or event has a physical cause. So, a baby is born. That event has a physical cause, the fertilization of the mother's ovum. Or the hard drive on a computer crashes. That event has a physical cause, the disintegration of one or more components of its hardware. Every physical object or event has a physical cause.

The principle of causal closure is a valid explanation when applied to physical phenomenon individually. It isn't a valid explanation when applied to physical phenomena collectively, the universe in other words. Something is true of the physical universe in general that isn't true of physical objects and events in particular. It too must have a cause but that cause can't be something physical because everything physical itself has a cause. Logic tells us that its cause must be uncaused, something that can be true only of a spiritual and self-existent being. That spiritual and self-existent being is the God of the Old and New Testaments, Yahweh. The universe and everything in it exists because He, the uncaused cause, created it.

He didn't just cause or create it though. He sustains it as well.

Paul was quick to point that out to the Greek philosophers in Acts 17:25, "He Himself gives to all people life and breath and all things." Think about all the bodily processes that together keep us alive and well, such as our pancreas producing insulin. Also think about all the physical processes that keep everything in the universe working the way it does, such as the so-called "laws of physics" that keep the earth orbiting around the sun. They are part of the "all things" about which Paul spoke to those philosophers. God not only created them; He also sustains them, that is, keeps them working the way they do. That's what Paul meant when He said of Jesus in Colossians 1:17 that "He is before all things, and in Him all things hold together." The anonymous author of Hebrews agreed. He wrote that Jesus "upholds all things by the word of His power." The verbs "holds together" and "upholds" are quite descriptive and conjure up thoughts of everyday bonding agents such as glue. Scientific journalist Robert Kunzig wrote an article about subatomic particles called gluons that are what he calls in its title "The Glue that Holds the World Together."[9] But according to Paul and the author of Hebrews, it's in finality Jesus not gluons who is the glue that holds the world together. In my view, the universe being sustained is as compelling an argument for a self-existent Creator as it existing in the first place is.

The God of the Bible is that Creator and it's His self-existence that most distinctly separates Him from all other realities. All things, including humans, are utterly dependent on His creating and sustaining work. They need Him to exist, if they're inanimate, or to live, if they're animate. But He, in stark contrast, is dependent on nothing. He needs no one else or nothing else to exist and live.

Self-existence Applied

The self-existence of God, if we understand it, fills us with awe. But it challenges us well. Since God alone is self-existent, He's the very ground of all existence and we must live as if He is.

It's here that we discover the root cause of all the behavioral problems that humans face both individually and culturally. That root cause is people living as if they, not God, are the ground of existence. A.W. Tozer's incisive words speak volumes: "Sin has many manifestations but its essence is one. A moral being, created to worship before the throne of God, sits on the throne of his own selfhood and from that elevated position declares, 'I AM.' That is sin in its concentrated essence . . ."[10] With the words "I AM," Tozer was referring back to God's personal name in Exodus 3:14 and His self-existence. The fact is that most of the seven billion people walking around on planet earth constantly think, feel, and act in practice as if they're the great "I am," that is, the ground of existence. They take themselves not God primarily into account in whatever the day-to-day circumstance or issue is before them.

I speak from experience here. Take something as simple as worship services from a pastoral perspective. For too many years of my ministry, I judged the success or failure of worship services by what the congregation thought about them. That was my chief concern in fact. Why? It was because worship services are a reflection on the pastor and I wanted people to think highly of me. For much of my ministry, in other words, I made worship services primarily about me and only secondarily about God.

My self-idolatry in doing so is a microcosm of the human condition. Most of us live as if we're the "I am," the ground of existence. We regularly take ourselves not God primarily into account in the circumstances and issues before us.

But God, not we, is the great "I am" and we need to think, feel, and act in day-to-day practice as if He is.

The founders of Alcoholics Anonymous, William Wilson and Robert Smith, understood probably as well as anyone how desperate this need of ours is. Describing what alcoholics must do, they wrote, "And first of all, we had to quit playing God" and then allow God to "play God."[11] That's the salient insight of AA that Ernest Kurtz's authoritative book on the group highlights in its title, *Not-God*. His title insinuates that "not-God" stands as the primary hurdle that addicted persons must get over. They thinking they're God, he contended, is their core problem and it must be overcome.

But it isn't just the core problem of alcoholics is it? Our need to quit playing God and to allow God to play God is as desperate as the alcoholic's. We too must regard Him and respond to Him as if He's the ground of existence.

We do so as a practical matter by taking Him primarily into account in whatever the circumstance or issue is before us. Promoted or fired. Win or lose. Praised or criticized. Healthy or ill. Boom or bust. Married or divorced. Rich or poor. Insured or uninsured. Whatever the circumstance or issue is, we direct our focus and action to glorifying Him, that is, *pleasing* and *esteeming Him*.

A middle-aged Christian friend of mine was dying of cancer. Her chief point of focus and action was what she called "dying for Jesus" or what the Puritans called "holy dying." She vocalized and pursued her overriding purpose to die joyously and courageously so that the faith of others in Jesus and their love for Him would increase. She lived as if He not she is God and died in the same way. She made her dying primarily about Him and secondarily about her loved ones and her.

Rick Warren began his best-selling book, *The Purpose Driven Life*, with the magnetic words, "It's not about you." He was right. Life is primarily about God and only secondarily about others and us. It's a keen insight that suggests the vigorous implication of God's self-existence to us. I'd summarize this implication by posing two fill-in-the blank questions. #1 – Human life is about ____. #2 – My life is about . The wrong answers are "Human life is about <u>humans</u>" and "My life is about <u>me</u>." The right answers are "Human life is about <u>God</u>" and "My life is about <u>God</u>." Those are the wrong and right answers because others and we are not the ground of existence. He is! He's self-existent and unlike everyone and everything else that exists, not made.

CHAPTER 5

"TIMELESS"

God Is Eternal

Our third attribute of God is inseparably linked with the second. Since He's self-existent, He's necessarily eternal as well.

God Is Eternal Revealed

The Bible uses just that term to depict Him. In Deuteronomy 33:27, for instance, Moses pronounces to the Israelites that "the *eternal* God is a dwelling place." The famous Christmas prophecy in Isaiah 9:6 names the child to be born as the "Eternal Father," a title that means possessor of eternity. Paul precipitates a doxology of praise in 1 Timothy 1:17 by describing God as "the King *eternal*." To deny that God is eternal is to reject the Bible's unequivocal witness that He is.

God Is Eternal Explained

God's own description of Himself in Revelation 1:8 as the One "who is and who was and who is to come" assists us in defining His eternal nature. He had no beginning and will never have an end. There has never been a time when He was not and there will never be a time when He will not be.

He has always existed, exists now, and always will exist. He's eternal!

But everything else, including us, is temporal, which thrusts us into the realm of time and prompts us to ponder how this eternal nature of His relates to time. He Himself reveals how it does in a series of three metaphors in Revelation 1:8, 21:6, and 22:13 that are synonymous in meaning. He states in those texts that He is the "Alpha and the Omega" (the first and last letters of the Greek alphabet), the "beginning and the end," and "the first and the last" – *at the same time*. Think of these metaphors as they relate to a baseball game. It begins with the first pitch and ends three hours or so later with the last. As temporal creatures attending the game, you and I experience the first pitch and *then* or *after that*, three hours or so later, the last. But God, as an eternal being, experiences the first pitch and the last *at the same time*. God's metaphors presuppose that He is not the beginning and *then* or *after that* the end, but the beginning and the end *at the same time*.

In doing so, they establish the relationship of God to time. He's timeless, that is, unrestricted by it. Asking and answering two questions helps un-muddy the waters of our understanding here. First, did time always exist? No, it did not. It had a beginning. That it did leads to a second question. When did it begin? It began in Genesis 1:1 when God created the material universe. Time did not exist. God created. Time then existed. It's a creation of His in other words. We must understand that in order to understand Him. He isn't a creature of time as you and I are. He's the creator of it. Consequently, He transcends it. He isn't *in* it but *apart from* it. It doesn't govern Him. He governs it as He wills.

Wayne Grudem aptly defines God's governance of time this way: "God has no beginning, end, or succession of moments in His own being, and he sees all time equally vividly, yet God sees events in time and acts in time."[12] He's right that God has no "succession of moments." Our individual lives come to us moment-by-moment but His doesn't. It's mind-numbing but true. Moments don't come and go for Him. For Him, there has always been and there will always be only a present moment.

That means He never actually remembers or anticipates anything. He always has and always will experience the past, the present, and the future at the same time, which is "right now."

Think about all the moments between the beginning of creation in Genesis 1:1 and the present moment. God experiences each of them, including the moment of your birth and mine, right now as you read this sentence. Think about all the moments between the present moment and the moment Jesus comes again. God experiences each of them, including the moment of your death and mine, right now.

That means that what to us "has happened" or "will happen" to God "is happening." Or to say it another way, "now" is the only time word that pertains to Him. There is no past or future to Him, no yesterday or tomorrow; only a never ending "now." In short, He's eternal and, therefore, timeless!

God Is Eternal Applied

You and I would have no relationship with Him if He weren't. The heart of the New Testament gospel is that you and I can have an ongoing and interactive relationship with the living God. The eternal and timeless nature of God, as much as any other attribute of His, makes it possible.

A Christian was struggling in her life with God and explained to me why. It dawned on her as she was praying one night that millions of others were too. "So how can God hear all of those prayers at once," she asked, leading her to broadly conclude, "God doesn't have time for me."

It's a valid issue that reflective Christians sooner or later raise and seek to resolve. Does God have time for us? Those who perceive Him as a creature of time subject to the same limitations it imposes upon us believe He doesn't.

Let's ruminate on how much time we *have* – not *had* or *will have* but *have*. It's the "present moment." But what is that present moment really? We can ask it a different way. What is the smallest measurable unit of time? I'd quickly discard one husband's claim that it's "the amount of time my wife is quiet." The high tech clocks commonly used in sporting events measure it in tenths of a second but in day-to-day practice, it's usually a second. That's our practical experience as creatures of time. Life comes to us as a succession of present moments or seconds that quickly pass.

Unless we're stranded alone on a desert island somewhere, a substantial percentage of those moments is necessarily devoted to relationships with others. Relationship consists of attending to and acting upon others, which takes time. So, when a little daughter scrapes her knee and cries, daddy devotes to her whatever present moments holding her, consoling her, and dressing the scrape requires. Or when an attorney makes partner, his friend devotes to him whatever present moments a celebratory dinner with him requires. Relationships, as we know all too well, take time and the greater the number of those relationships or the greater their intimacy the more time they take.

But we're creatures of time. All we have are the quickly passing succession of moments coming to us, which determines both the number and the intimacy of the relationships of which we're capable. We don't have enough present moments to attend to and act upon everyone. We must be discriminating in to whom we relate and to what extent we relate to them. That partially explains, for instance, why God in the Bible endorses monogamy and disparages polygamy. Marriage is a reflex of the Trinity and requires a measure of "attending to" and "acting upon" that's unique to it. When it comes to spouses, in other words, we only have time for one. You get the point I'm making I'm sure. Our time limitations translate into relationship limitations.

Unfortunately, it's common for Christians to project those same limitations of ours on to God. They conclude that He couldn't possibly attend to and act upon the countless details of the lives of the seven billion people who inhabit planet earth. Failing to understand what it means that He's eternal and timeless, they conclude that He "doesn't have time for me."

But He does because, as we learned, He isn't *in* time as we are. As its creator, He's *apart* from it and not subject to it.

He's timeless so that every moment of time that lasts a second for us never ends for Him.

An imperfect analogy may be helpful in "getting a handle" on this remarkable reality. When you watch a movie on a DVD, you're outside the activities and events in it and thus its time as well. Suppose it's a romance and when the two protagonists kiss, you press the pause button on the controller. To them, the kiss at the point you paused it lasts a moment. But to you, it lasts as long as you please. It may be a minute, an hour, a day, a month, or more. You govern the very time that binds them. It's somewhat like that for God.

The Bible makes astonishing claims about the personal nature of His involvement with His created world and the humans who inhabit it. In Psalm 56:6, for example, David acknowledges to God that "You have taken account of my wanderings; put my tears in Your bottle." This text by way of example and many others establish God's connectedness of concern with humans. He attends to and acts upon all of us in all of the particulars of our lives, from the most important of those to the least.

And it's His eternal and timeless nature that enables Him to do so. When a child scrapes her knee and sheds a tear, the moment in which she does never ends for Him. He has an eternity of time not just a second of time to attend to her misfortune. When a million people pray at once, the moment in which they do never ends for Him. He has an eternity of time not just a second of time to attend to their requests. More generally, He always has an eternity of time not just a second of time to attend to every particular activity, experience, and event of every person's life – and He does.

The ramification is profound. Imagine something. You are the only creature that God made and the only one to whom He gives His attention and care. He attends to you and acts upon you as if it's just Him and you alone. That is in fact the practical consequence of His eternal and timeless nature. He always has all the time in the world for you and gives it.

CHAPTER 6

"1+1+1=1"

God Is Triune

Calculate the sum in the following equation: 1+1+1=? Even the most mathematically challenged persons among us can. The sum is "3." Or is it? It depends on the context. In mathematics, 1+1+1 always equals "3." But in the metaphysics of God, 1+1+1 equals "1" because He's triune.

God Is Triune Revealed

The words "trinity" and "triune" are so frequently used in our Christian communities that they're familiar to us all. As Jehovah's Witnesses are quick to bring to our attention though, the Bible uses neither word. A church father named Tertullian was the first person known to have used the word "trinity" in relation to God in 170 A.D. Jehovah's Witnesses take this to be a consequential historical fact that bears heavily on the Trinity debate, but it doesn't. It's actually irrelevant to it because while the Bible doesn't use the words "trinity" and "triune," it's unambiguous in teaching the reality behind them.

Suppose we read the Bible for the first time with no knowledge of Christianity. We'd recognize if we did that it elevates three persons above all the rest: God (also called the

"Father"), the Son, and the Holy Spirit. In Matthew 28:19, for instance, it exhorts us to make disciples of all the nations, baptizing them in the name of "the Father, Son, and Holy Spirit." Or in Jude 20-21, it challenges us to keep ourselves in "the love of God," to wait for the mercy of "our Lord Jesus Christ," and to pray "in the Holy Spirit." Those two are just samplings of texts that give eminence to persons it calls the Father, Son, and Holy Spirit.

It doing so, if we were to give it deeper thought, would raise a question in our minds. Who are these three persons and what makes them special? The word "Father" obviously refers to God, but who are the Son and the Holy Spirit? We easily discern from the texts in which they appear that they aren't humans. They're obviously supernatural persons but what kind of supernatural persons? We'd exegete (critically interpret) relevant texts about Jesus and the Holy Spirit to find out.

The relevant texts about Jesus include the following: Romans 9:5; 1 Corinthians 2:16; 8:6; 1 Thessalonians 3:11; 2 Thessalonians 1:8; 2:16; 1 Timothy 1:1-2; Titus 2:13; 3:4; 3:6; Hebrews 1:2; 1:8; 1:10-12; 2 Peter 1:1; and Revelation 1:17; 5:8; and 5:13. Exegeting those texts teaches us something startling about Him. He's God. Hebrews 1:8 illustrates what I mean. The Sons of Korah prophesied the coming of the Messiah in Psalm 45:6, saying of Him that "Your throne, O God, is forever and ever." The author of Hebrews quotes those exact words in verse 8 as referring to "the Son," Jesus. The Sons of Korah and the author of Hebrews, in other words, address Jesus as God. Hebrews 1:8 is characteristic of the verses listed with it. Their constructions reveal either explicitly or implicitly that Jesus is God.

But what about the Holy Spirit? Who is He?

The relevant texts about Him include what I call "identity exchanges." In one kind of identity exchange, a part of a text speaks as if it's God that's acting or being acted upon and another part of it as if it's the Holy Spirit acting or being acted upon. In Acts 5:3, it's stated that Ananias lied "to the Holy

Spirit." In the next verse, 4, it's stated that he lied "to God." In another kind of identity exchange, a text states that God is acting or being acted upon and another related text states that it's the Holy Spirit who is acting or being acted upon. Jeremiah 31:33-34 records what "the LORD" (Yahweh) says about the Israelites. A related text, Hebrews 10:15-17, quotes both verses but attributes what Yahweh says in them to the Holy Spirit. You can see from the two examples of identity exchanges I just gave they treat God and the Holy Spirit as if they're one and the same because they are.

So do what theologians call "Triadic formulas," statements that mention the Father, Son, and Holy Spirit together in parallel constructions. Paul closes out his second letter to the Corinthian church with his desire that "The grace of the Lord Jesus Christ, and the love of God, and the fellowship of the Holy Spirit, be with you all." Triadic formulas like this one don't prove the unity and equality of the three persons but do suggest it. One, however, comes close to proving it. It's the baptismal formula I mentioned in Matthew 28:19, "in the name of the Father and the Son and the Holy Spirit." Notice that its "name" singular as opposed to the plural "names" that we'd expect, intimating a unity and equality of their nature. Triadic formulas point us to the Trinitarian nature of God and thus, the deity of the Holy Spirit.

So do texts that ascribe attributes of God to Him. Hebrews 9:14, which designates Him as "the eternal Spirit" is one of those. Recall from Chapter Five that God alone of all realities is eternal. Since the Holy Spirit is eternal, therefore, He must be God. 1 Corinthians 2:10-11 ascribes another attribute of God to Him, omniscience. This text, because it establishes the divinity of the Holy Spirit more than any other, demands a closer look.

Verse 10 mentions the Holy Spirit and discloses about Him that He "searches" what Paul calls "the depths of God." The Greek word translated "depths" connotes the unfathomable things of God. Can any finite creature including preeminent spiritual beings such as angels search or know the depths of God? No, they cannot just because they're finite. Only an infinite (limitless) being could know them. But the Holy Spirit does just that, indicating that He's infinite. Since only God of all realities is infinite, the Holy Spirit must be God.

Paul proceeds to use an analogy in verse 11 to explain why the Holy Spirit is able to do what He does in verse 10. The only one who can know the deepest thoughts of a human person is the person himself. In the same way, Paul says in verse 11, the only one who can know the deepest thoughts of God is God Himself, which the Holy Spirit knows. It necessarily follows then that the Holy Spirit must be God Himself.

At this point, we've examined enough relevant texts to draw two firm conclusions. The Father, the Son, and the Holy Spirit are the three dominant of all realities, and each is God. But we also conclude, based on Deuteronomy 6:4 and other related texts, that God is "one." Tying those conclusions together, we recognize that God is one but three or as Tertullian said it, He's triune

God Is Triune Explained

Understanding the Trinitarian nature of God begins with two Biblical revelations about the Father, Son, and Holy Spirit. One is that each possesses the qualities or traits of personhood. Each is self-conscious and self-directing – thinking, feeling, willing, and relating to each other and to creation. Each is a real live person in other words and in that sense is separate from the other two. As I've already noted, the other Biblical revelation is that the Father, the son, and the Holy Spirit are somehow synonymous. That somehow is that they are one in substance or essence.

Those are two Biblical revelations and we can infer from them the impenetrable truth about God. He is one being with three persons. It bears repeating since it's the traditional explanation of His triune nature. He is one being with three persons. The three persons together comprise one being,

Yahweh, making Him what C.S. Lewis called "superpersonal" – something more than a mere person.

The celebrated 4th century *Athanasian Creed*, the longest of the standard Christian creeds and a classic statement on the Trinity, adds to our comprehension. It describes God as follows: "But the Catholic faith is this, that we venerate one God in Trinity, and the Trinity in oneness; neither confounding the persons, nor dividing their substance for there is one person of the Father, another of the Son, and another of the Holy Spirit but the divine nature of the Father and of the Son and of the Holy Spirit is one, their glory is equal, their majesty coeternal."

This section of the creed is a sort of broadside that corrects two related mistakes that Christians make. One is blurring the line between the three persons of the Godhead. We need to view them as three distinct persons not one person. The other is separating their substance. We need to view them as one being, not three.

Christians make another mistake that this section of the creed corrects. They think that one person of the Godhead, the Father, is more important than the other two. The word "equal" in the creed shows how misguided that point of view is. It rightly affirms that none of the three persons is greater than the other two in authority, competence, or character. Jesus did state in John 14:28 that "the Father is greater than I." Theologians in days gone by took the inequality of which He spoke to mean that He was equal to His Father in His Godhead but less than the Father in His manhood. That's exactly right. In His earthly body, Jesus was lesser than the Father and Holy Spirit in His position, as the God-man, but not in His person, as God. In truth, the Father, Son, and Holy Spirit are equal in authority, competence, and character.

It's helpful for the sake of clarity to think of their equality as it relates to their attributes. All the attributes of God that are identified, explained, and applied in this book belong to each of the three persons. Each one, for instance, is omnipotent and omniscient making them by definition equally powerful and knowing. Each one possesses the same perfect and infinite attributes as the other two with the result that they're ontologically equal.

The Christian Forums website posed a captivating topic of discussion called "the mathematics of the Trinity." You now know what the mathematics of the Trinity is: 1+1+1=3. The addends on the left side of the equation are the three persons of God. The sum on the right side is their one being. God is three persons with one being. It's what the Athanasian Creed calls the Trinity in Unity.

The Trinity in Unity is beyond our experience. We know or know of thousands of humans, each of whom is one person with one being. So, we cannot comprehend three persons with one being. Sects like Jehovah's Witnesses and Mormons delight in pointing this out and concluding from it that the doctrine of the Trinity is irrational. They're wrong! It isn't *irrational* or *contrary to* reason. It's *transrational* or *beyond* reason. Why don't we understand it? It isn't that it's defies logic; it's that it defies knowledge by experience and those are two entirely different things.

In his enduring book *Mere Christianity*, C.S. Lewis uses a simile that makes our plight more palatable to us. He contrasts our experience of personhood and God's in terms of one, two, and three dimensional worlds. In the one dimensional world, we can move in only one direction from right to left, restricting us to a straight line. In the two dimensional world, we can move in two directions, from right to left and up and down, enlarging our experience to figures such as a square or rectangle. Finally, in the three dimensional world, we can move in three directions, right to left, up and down, and in and out, enlarging our experience still to solid bodies such as a cube.[13]

Our experience of personhood and God's is like that. Our experience of one person and one being is like the one dimensional world and the simple straight line. God's experience of personhood is like the three dimensional world and the complex combinations that create solid bodies. Suppose people in the one dimensional world are told about a solid body, the cube. They couldn't process it, not because it isn't true that such bodies exist, but because they've never experienced it. It's like that with the Trinity and us. We can't process three persons who are one being not because it isn't true such a being exists but because we've never experienced it.

I say that to say this. The idea that God is triune isn't irrational but transrational just as the idea that He's eternal is. It doesn't defy logic. It defies knowledge by experience. We can with intellectual integrity embrace, defend, and promote the Trinitarian nature of God.

God Is Triune Applied

We can do so and we should, with urgency. I've come to a conclusion based on countless conversations with Christians over the years. Many operate under the assumption that our belief in the Trinity is substantially dogma. It's a tenet we have to believe to be Christians, but it doesn't really matter much practically that we do. Calling that assumption crooked thinking would be an understatement. The fact is that the Trinitarian nature of God and our grasp of it dramatically affect the persons we are and the day-to-day lives we lead.

The reason is a simple one. The fundamental characteristic of humans and human life is that they are in their psychological and social nature personal and they are that because God is Triune. Their personal nature is a reflex and reflection of His Trinitarian nature. Stated simply, we're relational creatures because the God who made us is a relational being. And He's a relational being because He's triune.

We "get" the connectedness of the "personal" with the "triune" by deliberating over a captivating question. Would God have a life if nothing else, spiritual or material, existed? If He is one being with one person as sects and heretics maintain, the answer is that He would not. Having a life requires something and or someone to act upon and interact with, which He wouldn't have if nothing else existed but Him. In reality though, He doesn't need anything else to exist in order to have a life because He's triune.

Jesus puts this issue to rest in John 17:24 by giving us a glimpse into what is perhaps the most intriguing of all truths about God. In His great intercessory prayer for His disciples of all generations, He asks God the Father that they "may see My glory which You have given Me, *for You loved me before the foundation of the world.*" Love inherently implies relationship between persons, in this case between God the Father and God the Son, and based on what we learned about Him, God the Holy Spirit as well. Before anything else existed, the three divine persons acted upon and interacted with each other and still do in a way that was and is intimate beyond our ability even to imagine it. The result was and is a life of perfect and limitless love and joy. God didn't create spiritual and material worlds and beings in order to experience love and joy. He created them to share the love and joy He already experienced from eternity. God always has had and always will have an utterly fulfilling communal life apart from His creation.

I use the word "communal" because it suggests the essence of the Trinitarian life. It's what we would call "community." The Trinity is God in community and what a glorious community it is. No human description could possibly do justice to the splendor of it but Dallas Willard's is rousing nonetheless. He writes that the Godhead is "a self-sufficing community of unspeakably magnificent personal beings of boundless, love, knowledge, and power."[14] I would add that because the Father, the Son, and the Holy Spirit are perfect in all respects, so is the community they form. Its perfection manifests itself in three ways.

The first, as we've learned, is in equality. It's widely held and taught that the Son and the Holy Spirit are subordinated to the Father but they aren't. Returning to the Athanasian Creed, the reality is that "in this Trinity, nothing is before or after, nothing is greater or less: but all three Persons coeternal, together, and equal." Since the three Persons are equal in nature or attributes, none has greater authority, influence, or importance than the other two.

The perfection of the Trinitarian community manifests itself in another way, others-centeredness. Each person of the Trinity is absorbed with pleasing and esteeming the other two. Cornelius Platinga captures something of this Trinitarian dynamic in his book *Engaging God's World*: "At the center of the universe, self-giving love is the dynamic currency of the Trinitarian life of God. The persons within God exalt each other, commune with each other, defer to one another. Each person, so to speak, makes room for the other two."[15] Well said and texts such as John 7:18; 13:31-32; 16:13-15; 17:4-5; and 17:22, 24 confirm it. The attention and action of each Person of the Trinity is on and for the other two.

There's a third way the perfection of the Trinitarian community manifests itself. It's in oneness. In *Paradise Lost*, John Milton pictures the Father and Son discussing the redemption of man with each other, their conversation wrongly implying that they could disagree or have different points of view about something. They could not. The Father, the Son, and the Holy Spirit possess a complete oneness of will with each other. They never debate things because they never disagree. They always concur instantly and without effort instead.

The equality, others-centeredness, and oneness that the Trinitarian community embodies bespeak its splendor. They impress upon us that C.S. Lewis wasn't exaggerating when he used the term "superpersonal" of the Godhead.

Keeping in mind that superpersonal nature of His, we turn our thoughts to the foundational principle I mentioned before. God always expresses His nature in what He creates, including our material world. And the most noticeable expression of His triune nature is humans in community. It's in us, in our psychological makeup, to have relationships that are meaningful and deep. We thrive when we do and languish when we don't. As Aristotle stated with keen insight in *Politics*, "But whoever is unable to live in society, or who has no need of it because he is sufficient for himself, must be either a beast or a god."[16] Aristotle was right and we know why. We're relational beings who form communities of human persons because God is Himself a community of divine persons. Simply put, human communities are a *reflex* of the Trinity that He intends to *reflect* the Trinity. They are imperfect reproductions of the Trinitarian community that are meant to point us to it, to show us what it's like. Two of those communities, rightly ordered, reflect the Trinitarian community more vividly than any of the rest.

One of those finds its roots in the intercessory prayer of Jesus in John 17. In verses 22-23, He asks Father God to make His disciples "one, just as we are one" and "perfected in unity." The thrust of His request is that Father God will reproduce the divine community in the persons of His disciples, a request that He granted on the Day of Pentecost in Acts 2. He reproduced it by creating a community on earth that Jesus and the New Testament writers called "the church," also called the body of Christ and the family of God. The church, as Jesus' request shows, is a reflex and a reflection of the Trinity. God doesn't save individuals only to save individuals. He saves individuals to form a community on earth that He Himself inhabits and sustains and that will continue forever in heaven. This community on earth is embodied in every local church around the world.

The words of Jesus in John 17:22 that His disciples and friends "may be one, just as We are one" reveal the church's overriding characteristic. Empowered and drawn together by the Triune God who inhabits them, its members routinely act upon and interact with each other as the Father, the Son, and the Holy Spirit do with each other. They form a Trinitarian community in which the three characteristics that epitomize the community of God epitomizes theirs as well.

First, equality prevails among them. Someone asked sculptress Sally Farnum's little daughter which of her mother's children her mother loved the best. To which she replied:

"She loves Jimmy the best because he's the oldest. She loves Johnny the best because he's the youngest. And she loves me the best because I'm her only girl." Kids say the darndest things and here the profoundest as well. Disciples and friends of Jesus believe and behave that same way. They regard and treat no one in a lesser or better way than anyone else. They regard and treat each one the best, making the church a truly egalitarian community on earth. In belief and practice, there is equality for all.

A second characteristic of the Trinitarian community prevails in the church. It's others-centeredness. The concentrated focus of each disciple or friend of Jesus is on the others, each seeking the glory and pleasure of the others over his or her own. Shirl Hoffman identifies how others-centeredness plays out in practice this way: "The Christian is exhorted to 'love others as you love yourself,' but far greater emphasis is placed on self-denial in order to ensure the welfare of others. The Christian's duty is to bestow honor on others, seek their advancement recognize their superiority, and show esteem for their gifts."[17]

Oneness is a third characteristic of the Trinitarian community that prevails in the church. Disciples and friends of Jesus, just because they're limited and flawed, can never achieve the perfect oneness of will that the Father, the Son, and the Holy Spirit have. But they achieve something like it as they're bound together by the divine presence among and in them. Rupertus Meldenius, a 17th century German theologian, coined a guiding principle for oneness in a tract he wrote during the Thirty Years War: "In the essentials unity; in the non-essentials liberty; in all things love." His motto has been officially adopted by several Christian groups including the Moravian Church of North America and the Evangelical Presbyterian Church. It also unofficially guides countless church communities that live it out in the presence and power of the Triune God.

Imagine an all-inclusive community comprised of people who could be counted upon to think and act with equality, others-centeredness, and oneness. It would be a circle of sufficiency marked by the absence of harm and the presence of help. The church, rightly ordered, is just that kind of community and as such, is a pointer to the Trinity.

There's a second earthly community that most vividly reflects the Trinitarian community. It's revealed in the Song of Solomon, a book that records the courtship of a man and woman madly in love with each other (1:9). Many Bible commentators and most Christians interpret the Song of Solomon to be an allegory about the love of God for His people. But it isn't. It's the one book in the Bible that God devotes exclusively to love and sex in marriage. The book's theme, in 8:6, states about love and sex in marriage that "Its flashes are flashes of fire, the very flame of Yahweh."

Solomon uses two metaphors here. One is that the flashes of love and sex in marriage are flashes of fire. The Hebrew word translated "flashes" connotes intensity and energy. The intensity and energy of love and sex in marriage are like the intensity and energy of fire. The other metaphor is that flashes of love and sex in marriage are the very flame of Yahweh. The intensity and energy of love and sex in marriage are like the intensity and energy of relationship in the Trinitarian community.

Those metaphors together teach us that love and sex in marriage are a reflex of God's Trinitarian nature. The Father, the Son, and the Holy Spirit reproduced the intensity and energy of their spiritual union and love most vividly in the sexual aspect of a marriage between one husband and one wife who are "madly" in love with each other. That in turn makes love and sex in marriage a reflection or what I would call "a testimony" of God's Trinitarian nature. They point, no matter how imperfectly, to the depth and dynamism of the Trinitarian union and love. The one thing on earth that most closely resembles the intensity and energy of the Trinitarian community is the sexual union of a husband and wife whose love for each other is permanent and exclusive. It, even more so than the church in community, is the most vigorous of all testimonies to the Trinity.

The implications of Song of Solomon 8:6 are far reaching.

One of those is that sexual union outside of marriage in a relationship that isn't permanent and exclusive is inconsistent with God's Trinitarian nature and thus a sin. What is beautiful and glorifying of God inside of marriage is vile and demeaning of Him outside of it. We need to expose the lie of so-called "casual sex." There is in reality nothing casual about it. Sexual union outside of marriage and inappropriate sex inside it always have dramatic and destructive physical, psychological, and most of all spiritual effects. The most destructive of those is that they defame God by trivializing the Trinitarian community. That's the most affecting consequence of all the sexual sin we observe in the sex-saturated culture around us. It defames God by trivializing the Trinitarian community. Sexual purity on the other hand glorifies Him by taking the Trinitarian community seriously. Making sure that the intensity and extent of our physical intimacy matches the intensity and extent of our relational commitment, with sexual union reserved for marriage, respects the Trinitarian nature of God and is a testimony of it.

Another vital implication of Song of Solomon 8:6 goes to marriage itself. A marriage testifies of God's Trinitarian nature only when it's joyful and passionate. Don't take my word for it. Take the wise man's in Proverbs 5:19. Referring to their wives, he calls on husbands to "be exhilarated always with her love." The Hebrew word translated "exhilarated" is also used in the Old Testament to describe the effects of strong drink. A good translation is "intoxicated always with her love." Franz Delitzsch's interpretation of the verse is eye-opening: "He speaks here of a morally permissible love–ecstasy . . . of an intensity of love connected with the feeling of superabundant happiness . . . to be wholly captivated by her, so that one is no longer in his own power, can no longer restrain himself."[18] It's a stirring reality that extends to wives as well. God wants and expects husbands and wives to be "drunk with love" for each other as we say it.

He wants and expects it no matter how long they've been married. The wise man points that out to his young male pupils in Proverbs 5:18b. When they're old, they should "rejoice in the wife of your youth." Husbands and wives should be just as drunk with love for each other in their old age as they were when they were courting.

Such passionate and joyful marriage that points to the Trinity doesn't happen fortuitously. It's a purposeful choice spouses make. A Christian education director of many years frequently advises young people to "fake it until you feel it." That slogan of his reflects a profound psychological reality. Feelings follow actions, including feelings of love. Love is created and nurtured by its expression. Functional people who persistently do loving things will eventually have loving feelings. Those loving feelings in the marriage relationship include passion and joy, opening up the course of Trinitarian marriages to us. In the power of the divine presence, we make and carry out the decision to steadily do loving things for our spouses. Loving feelings of passion and joy will follow if we do and our marriages will be robust testimonies of the Trinity.

The church and marriage evidence that the Trinitarian nature of God is more than a test of orthodoxy. It's an explanation of our communal lives and how they should proceed. All of our personal relationships, especially our ecclesiastical and marital ones, are a reflex of the Trinity and at their best a reflection of it. May we do our part to make them just that.

CHAPTER 7

"EVERYPLACE AT ONCE"

God Is Omnipresent

In the movie *A Walk to Remember*, a young man fulfills a young woman's wish to be in two places at once by having her straddle the state line. The scene was cute but for the more realistic among us inaccurate as well. Straddling a state line or any other boundary doesn't constitute being in two places at once. It's the best we can do though because no bodily creature can be in two places at once. We often wish we could, when we have too many things to do, but we can't. We are always, at every moment of our lives, in one place at once. We're localized, in other words, restricted to one place at a time.

But God is not. On the contrary, He isn't in just two places at once but everyplace at once, which introduces a fifth attribute of His. He's omnipresent.

God Is Omnipresent Revealed

In his prayer of dedication in 1 Kings 8, Solomon was quick to acknowledge that God manifesting His presence at the newly built temple didn't mean He was only there. He espoused God's omnipresence by insisting in verse 27 that "the highest heaven cannot contain You, how much less this house which I have built." The word "contain" is graphic. Imagine trying to pour all the water from the Great Lakes into a glass. Just as the water from the Great Lakes would fill and overflow the glass, so God's presence fills and overflows the entire universe itself.

Solomon's father David was as impressed by God's omnipresence as he was. In Psalm 139:7, David asked two rhetorical questions, the implied answer to which is that we can't "go" or "flee" from God's presence. A country song asks in its title "If You Leave Me, Can I Go with You?" According to verse 7, if that title was about God and us, it would be "If You Leave Me, I'll Be Where You Go." David drives that point home in verse 8 by mentioning the two places that in the ancient mind were furthest apart, Sheol and Heaven. God is in both of those places at once he writes.

Paul the Apostle took the thought of David and Solomon a step further in Acts 17:27-28. In verses 22-26, he depicts the one true God to a group of Greek philosophers, proclaiming about Him in verse 28, "for in Him we live and move and exist." He was speaking literally in spatial terms not metaphorically. Take a deep breath. The air that you take into your lungs comes from the space immediately around you. Our moment by moment experience is one of living, moving, and existing in air. In the same way, God inhabits all the space immediately around us so that we live, move, and exist as immersed in His presence as we are in air.

These texts and others drive away any doubts we may have in our minds. God is omnipresent.

God Is Omnipresent Explained

The component parts of the word "omnipresent" define it for us. According to *Dictionary.com*, the word "present" denotes "being here" and the prefix "omni" denotes "everywhere." Putting the word and its prefix together connotes that to be omnipresent is to be "here" everywhere. You, where you are at this moment, can correctly say that God in the entirety of His being is "here." At the same time, I where I am can correctly say that God in the entirety of His being is "here" no matter how far from you I am. He isn't localized as you and I and everything material are. Think of what one website for children calls "location words" such as "above," "behind," "around," "beneath," "down," "in," "in front of," "inside," "middle," and "outside." The fullness of God's presence encompasses those and all locations no matter where they are. He is always everywhere present with His entire being at the same time.

That "everywhere" includes all *places*. It's estimated that there are 100,000,000,000,000,000,000 planets in the universe. Contemplate the total number of places on those planets. There are so many that we couldn't conceive let alone count them. Nevertheless, God is in the fullness of His being always in those places and all places at once.

"Everywhere" also includes all *space*. According to some astronomers, the universe is approximately 27 billion light years across. One light year equals 5,880,000,000,000 miles. Multiply that number by 27 billion and that's how many miles across the universe is. It's a mind-blowing number that exposes most of the universe for what it is, space. But none of it is empty. We thoughtlessly talk about "empty space." In truth though, there's no such thing. It's all filled with the presence of God. He always inhabits every square inch of space in the universe including the space immediately around us with His entire being at once.

Were now able to encapsulate what it means that God is omnipresent. He is always present with His entire being in every place and in every square inch of space at the same time.

But I'm speaking figuratively in saying that. To enhance our ability to understand and communicate, we say that God is present in places and space but it isn't literally true that He is. In reality, as Paul makes clear to the Greek philosophers in Acts 17:27-28, places and spaces are "in Him." Just as you and I are immersed in the air we breathe, so the universe and everything in it are immersed in the presence of God. Just as the air envelops us on all sides, so God's presence envelops the universe and everything in it on all sides. I know of no more fastidious summary of God's omnipresence than A.W. Tozer's: "In His infinitude He surrounds the finite creation and contains it. There is no place beyond Him for anything to be. God is our environment as the sea is to the fish and the air to the bird."[19]

God Is Omnipresent Applied

Depending on our posture toward Him and His toward us, the omnipresence of God is either the most unsettling or encouraging of all His attributes. It is so because of its moment by moment repercussion. We have no right to privacy.

While the U.S. Constitution provides no express right to privacy, the U.S. Supreme Court held in a series of decisions that a penumbra of various Bill of Rights guarantees creates a "zone of privacy" upon which government can't infringe. An impassioned proponent of the right to privacy, Supreme Court Justice Louis Brandeis, defined it as the "the right to be let alone."

That's what we want isn't? It's to be let alone to do whatever we desire without being observed and assessed by government or anyone else for that matter. But in relation to God, because of His omnipresence, we don't get that. In relation to Him, there is no right to privacy and in the course of our daily lives, no privacy at all. We are literally never alone. He is always with us every second of every day of our lives, observing and assessing us.

An eye-catching anthropomorphism, excuse the play on words, broadcasts just that reality to us. In 2 Chronicles 16:9, Hanani the prophet informed King Asa that "the eyes of the LORD move to and fro throughout the earth." The wise man concurs in Proverbs 15:3 by affirming that "The eyes of the LORD are in every place." Think about what a person's eyes do. They observe with the result that the person knows what is observed. It's what we call being an "eyewitness." According to the anthropomorphism "the eyes of the LORD," that's what He is, a perpetual eyewitness.

Years ago, the IRS received an anonymous letter containing $400 cash and a confession. The sender stated that he had cheated on his taxes, felt remorse, and was making restitution. To this day, no one on earth knows who that person was. But God does. He was there and an eyewitness when the person both cheated and wrote the letter. The moral of the story is that we say and do nothing in private. He "observes" and knows it all and as the "eyes of the LORD" imply, assesses its rightness and wrongness in doing so.

It's disconcerting to humans that He does. The United States Supreme Court decisions unfolding the right to privacy reflect that its one of our culture's deepest concerns. People generally desire and demand it and there's an overriding reason they do. A mother discovered her little son doing what he knew he shouldn't, writing with a crayon on the wall. He was having so much fun though when he noticed her watching, he didn't stop but said instead, "Go away mommy." His honest response illustrates why people demand privacy. It's because it's essential to them that they be unobserved in the wrong they do. Others observing and knowing the bad things they do make them feel guilty, insecure, and even fearful. So, they demand privacy – to be left alone in doing it.

But they never get it because the One whose opinion counts the most is omnipresent. He's always with everyone observing, knowing, and assessing everything they say and do.

That's the reality and if we're wise, we'll act according to it. Lois Blanchard Eades wrote a thought-provoking poem titled "If Jesus Came to Your House" that teaches us how. Deliberate over an excerpt from it:

If Jesus came to your house to spend a day or two –
If He came unexpectedly, I wonder what you'd do . . . .
Would you go right on doing the things you always do?
Would you go right on saying the things you always say?
Would life for you continue as it does from day to day . . . .
Would you take Jesus with you everywhere you'd planned to go?
Or would you, maybe, change your plans for just a day or so . . . .
Would you be glad to have Him stay forever on and on?
Or would you sigh with great relief when He at last was gone?
It might be interesting to know the things that you would do
If Jesus Christ in person came to spend some time with you.[20]

Eades' poem is food for thought. Suppose Jesus appeared in bodily form and informed us that He was going to be with us 24 hours a day for the next week. Let's ask and answer two questions in that regard. Would we talk and act differently than we normally do? If so, would we go back to talking and acting the way we normally do when He left? If our answers to those questions are "yes" and "no" respectively, then one of three things is true about us. We don't understand the omnipresence of God, we understand it but don't believe it, or we understand and believe it but don't care.

The objective fact is that the Father, Son, and Holy Spirit are with us every moment of every day of our lives. Whether we like it or not, they never leave us. If there is something we wouldn't say or do in their presence, then we had better not say or do it because we're always in their presence. Examples abound. If the Father, the Son, or the Holy Spirit were with me in bodily form, would I watch the television show or movie I'm watching now, respond to the person who insulted me the way I'm responding now, buy the luxurious home I'm living in now, skip worship services on Sunday to attend little league games as I'm doing now, and so on. You get the idea. Only live the way we would – only say and do the things we would – if God was with us because He is.

There is a flip side to the coin of God's omnipresence. He not only assesses from the space right around us but assists us and protects us from there as well. His constant presence is as encouraging to the hard pressed as it can be unsettling to the iniquitous.

Psalm 91:1-10 is rich in promise of God's unceasing and personalized care of us. Verse 10 closes out the text with the summarizing statement that "No evil will befall you, nor will any plague come near your tent." Commentator Derek Kidner interprets the text to teach God's "versatile and individual protection" and offers the following synopsis of its message: "This is, of course, a statement of exact minute providence, not a charm against adversity . . . What it does assure us is that nothing can touch God's servant but by God's leave."[21] It's a bold promise that God can keep and His omnipresence is at the heart of His ability to do so.

When we calculate the dangers and threats that permeate our day-to-day world and lives in the form of bacteria and viruses, the carelessness of others, our own carelessness, evildoers, defective products, and accidents to name a few, it's literally a miracle that any of us reach adulthood "in one piece" as we say it. I'm struck, for instance, by how many cars have come hurtling down a two lane highway or street toward mine. It's been thousands in my forty one years of driving and yet, I've never had an accident. Many of you have the same experience and the question is "How do we explain it?" It's God's versatile and individual protection from the space right around us, and I emphasize that phrase, "from the space right around us."

Much of the anxiety in people's lives is the result of their failure to understand or believe this "at hand" presence of His.

The things they say, if we're attentive to them, betray the weakness of their faith or the crookedness of their thinking in that regard. I mentioned in Chapter 1, for instance, the popular billboard that depicts God saying "Don't make me come down there" as if He weren't already here on earth. Or people complain that "My prayers don't seem to be getting beyond the four walls," thinking they must for God to hear them because that's where He is – beyond the four walls. Or people lament that "I can't stand being alone," insinuating when they do that no one including God is with them.

Statements like those are reflective of where people believe God to be. He's in what Paul called "the heavenly places" and those heavenly places are far from us. He's "way out there" and there's a vast amount of space between Him and us and that space is empty. The consequence is He's far removed from our day-to-day lives and us. He does come to assist us here and there when we need it. But then when He's done assisting us, He returns to where He was – way out there someplace.

Thinking about God that way is dispiriting. It's as if we have a "long distance relationship" with Him that renders closeness and intimacy with Him psychologically impossible. It's also anxiety inducing. It's as if we're moving through this dangerous world and life of ours alone and vulnerable.

Closeness of relationship with God and peace of mind about the world we live in require that we think straight about the omnipresence of God. We learn the details of His "at hand" presence as presented in this chapter and then personalize them. So, we routinely bring to mind that He inhabits every square inch of space *around us* and that it's from the space right around us and not from above us or from beyond us that He relates to us, protects us, and assists us.

It's a life transforming point of view and I speak from experience. I remember my wife Jill being diagnosed with colon cancer as if it were yesterday. My very first thought when the surgeon informed us she had it was that God's presence filled the space around her and me and that we'd go through whatever came next immersed in it. Years ago, Helen Reddy sang about "You and me against the world, sometimes it seems like you and me against the world." It didn't seem that way to me through the next months of my wife's surgery, surgery complications, and chemotherapy – as if it were Jill and me against the cancer. With a strong sense of God's enveloping presence, it seemed as if it were He and Jill and me against it. And both of us had a transcendent experience of calmness and peace as a result. I've learned from that experience and countless others you and I and everyone else are never alone.

It's ironic, therefore, that loneliness is what social observers call a social epidemic or what Mother Teresa called the leprosy of the modern world. People feel alone, but it isn't because they are. It's because they ignore, deny, or don't know that the ultimate reality, the Triune and personal God, is in the entirety of His being everywhere at once, including with them. He is omnipresent!

CHAPTER 8

"POWER FULL"

God Is Omnipotent

F*orbes Magazine* published an article titled "4 Signs that You're Too Power Hungry." "Power hungry" is an appropriate metaphor to describe the human craving for power, which rivals the craving of a starving man for food. The hunger for power has been both a driving force in the development of Western civilization and an ongoing theme in its historical writings. Many people it seems can't get enough of it. God, in sharp contrast, isn't power hungry and never will be. He's "power full" instead. He's omnipotent!

God Is Omnipotent Revealed

The Bible celebrates the omnipotence of God from its first book through its last. Old Testament and New Testament saints alike reveled in this glorious attribute of His.

Abraham was one of those. When his wife Sarah and he were geriatrics, God promised she would give birth to a son. God responded to Sarah's skeptical laughter by asking Abraham a straight to the point rhetorical question, "Is anything too difficult for the LORD?" His implied answer that Abraham and Sarah came to know by experience in Genesis 21 was "No." Nothing is too difficult for Him including making a woman who is well past the age of child bearing able to bear one.

Jeremiah understood that and firmly believed it as well. Addressing God in prayer and having referred to His "great power" and "outstretched arm," he went on to conclude in Jeremiah 32:17 that "Nothing is too difficult for You."

In the climactic last chapter of the book that has his name, Job agreed, expressing his faith in God's power a bit differently. Having been spoken to by God in a long discourse about His greatness, Job replied in 42:2, "I know You can do all things."

Jesus concurred in Matthew 19:26 with a little different slant. Noting the limitations of human capability, "With people this is impossible," He proceeded to assert the limitlessness of divine capability, "but with God all things are possible."

John learned well from his master Jesus and espoused the omnipotence of God with one word. Describing a heavenly vision of his in Revelation 21:22, he designated "the Lord God" as "the *Almighty*."

There's no attribute of God that the Bible champions with more clarity than this. He's omnipotent!

God Is Omnipotent Explained

A logical place to start in defining the omnipotence of God is with a word the KJV Bibles uses of Him 56 times. The English translation of the Hebrew and Greek words is "almighty" as in the aforementioned verse, Revelation 21:22. According to *Helps Word Studies*, the Greek word translated that connotes "unrestricted power exercising unqualified dominion."[22] Personally, that's my favorite definition of "almighty" since it highlights both the nature of God's omnipotence and the purpose to which He directs it. He's all-powerful and sovereign. He possesses limitless power and uses it to exert complete mastery over all of reality in both the spiritual and material worlds.

God's omnipotence doesn't mean He can do anything. There are some things He can't do. My childhood pastor often posed the brain teasing question that's a favorite of many, "Can God make a rock so big He can't lift it?" The quandary is apparent to us all. If the answer is "Yes," there's something He can't do, lift the rock. If the answer is "No," there's also something He can't do, make a rock that big. It's a simple point well made. God cannot do illogical or contradictory things.

That He can't sheds light on an issue with which most of us have wrestled. I'll ask you what a parishioner once asked me, "Why doesn't God just make people love Him?" It would solve most of the world's problems wouldn't it if He could and did?

The problem is that He can't. By reason of its very nature love requires the freedom to care about and pursue the well-being of the beloved. That means the moment God "makes" someone love Him it's no longer love but compulsion. This explains partially the presence of evil in the world. God can't make a creature whether it's spiritual or bodily with the capacity to love without also making it with the capacity not to love. The first capacity, by definition, is necessarily intertwined with the second. The risk is obvious. The creature may choose not to love and instantaneously evil is born. According to the Biblical narrative, that's exactly what happened before creation when Satan "fell" and after it when Adam and Eve did as well. The presence of evil in real life is a constant reminder to us all. That God is omnipotent doesn't mean He can do anything.

It does mean He possesses limitless power or, as we more commonly say it, He's all-powerful. His power is quantitatively and qualitatively infinite.

One aspect of this infinite power of His is energy. In *The Divine Conspiracy*, Dallas Willard explains with his usual profundity that God has the "e" side of the "e=mc2" equation available to Him. He doesn't need matter as humans do to possess energy. It's an inherent part of His limitless power and is itself limitless, enabling Him to create all the matter that exists.[23]

Speaking of all the matter that exists, it's worth reflecting a moment on the total energy in it. In 2013, scientists detected a gamma ray burst from deep in space that was the largest ever recorded. A NASA website estimates that the energy beams from the blast equaled the energy output of 35 trillion of our suns. That gamma burst is just a metaphorical drop in the bucket of all the energy that exists in the universe, but as incalculable as the total energy in the universe is, it's miniscule compared to the limitless energy of its Creator.

This energy aspect of God's power alone is a sufficient basis for appreciating the awesomeness of that power. But our appreciation grows as we descend further into its details.

Recall Jeremiah's utterance about God's power in 32:17 of his prophetic book, "Nothing is too difficult for you." We do no injustice to the spirit of the text by removing the word "too." That's God's power is limitless necessarily means that *nothing is difficult for him*.

We can state it positively by identifying antonyms of the words "nothing" and "difficult." According to *Thesaurus.com*, antonyms for the word "difficult" include "easy," "effortless," "facile," "simple," "uncomplicated," "a breeze," "child's play," and "easy as pie" to name a few. The antonym of the word "nothing" is the word "everything." So stated positively, Jeremiah 32:17 teaches that everything is easy to God. Think of God's greatest material achievement. It's surely His creation of the universe. Now think of one of our simplest material or bodily achievements such as blinking our eyes. God creating the universe was easier for Him than blinking our eyes is for us. Creating the universe was child's play, a piece of cake, a breeze to Him. More accurately, He created the universe and did and does everything effortlessly.

The effortlessness of His actions is understandable in light of His infinite power. "Limitless" is an absolute word that leaves no wiggle room on either end of it for the words "more" and "less." Since God's power is limitless, He is always "power full," that is, full of power. He is never emptied of even the slightest amount of it. He has never possessed more or less of it. He didn't, for instance, possess more of it before creating the universe and less after creating it. He also never possesses more or less of it in His unceasing action of sustaining it. Whatever His action is, whether it's stopping the earth from rotating on its axis (Joshua 10:12-14) or making an iron ax head float (2 Kings 6:1-7), He always has the same power after doing it as He did before. All of His actions are effortless because His power is limitless.

And He puts it to use! Referring back to our definition of "almighty," He uses it to exercise unqualified dominion over the spiritual and material worlds He created. More particularly, He has the unqualified power to bend the ultimate foundations of all reality to His will and does.

Those foundations include what we call the "laws of nature." We learned a host of those in our high school science classes. One is the Law of Gravity that says what goes up must come down. However hard a major league baseball player hits a baseball, it eventually falls to the ground. Another is the First Law of Thermodynamics that says, in its simplest form, matter can be neither created nor destroyed. It may be shocking to us but it's true that every single atom that comprised Abraham Lincoln's body still exists. A third law is the Law of Buoyancy. Objects denser than the liquid in which they're placed will sink. Iron ax heads go to the bottom when they fall into water. Those three laws of nature are representative of the foundations of physical reality.

The word "laws" though is misleading. It suggests that they govern the universe – that they direct how things work – but they don't. What we call laws of nature aren't laws at all. They're simply descriptions of God's power at work. He acts in nature in a specific and uniform way and we call it a "law." So, when a baseball player hits a 475 foot home run, it eventually coming down isn't the law of gravity at work. It's God at work "upholding all things by the word of His power"

(Hebrews 1:3). The bottom line is that laws of nature are at their core uniform actions of God.

Nevertheless, God is sovereign and uses His power as He wills. While He normally acts uniformly in upholding the universe, He isn't bound to and sometimes doesn't. He sometimes acts differently, out of the ordinary so to speak, so that what we call "miracles" occur.

One of my favorite narratives in the Bible is that of the borrowed iron ax head in 2 Kings 6:1-7. It came off the handle as it was being used and pursuant to the uniform action of God, sank to the bottom. Responding to the borrower's distress and His prophet's request, however, God acted differently at that particular time and place in the universe and caused what normally sinks to float. The awesomeness of His power in doing so is usually lost in the banality of the scene, but it's there for those of us who have eyes that see.

The floating ax head is just one piece in the mass of Biblical and empirical evidence that God possesses limitless power and uses it to exercise dominion over everything He's made. He's omnipotent or power full and sovereign.

God Is Omnipotent Applied

And He uses that power on behalf of His people. Paul acknowledged as much in Ephesians 1:19 citing "the surpassing greatness of His power toward us who believe." Peter stated it just as strongly if not more so in 1:3 of his Second Letter, "His divine power has granted to us everything pertaining to life and godliness." The author of Hebrews adds the further insight in 6:5 of his book that disciples of Jesus "have tasted . . . . the powers of the age to come." These texts make an audacious claim. Experiencing God's power enables us to live an "age to come" or eternal kind of life right now. In light of those texts, you and I as disciples of Jesus can live our day-to-day lives with the firm conviction that God is putting His power to work on our behalf as we do.

He does so in two ways.

First, His power works in us to transform what we are. Knowing that it does, Paul prays for the Christians at Ephesus that God will grant them "to be strengthened with power through His Spirit in the inner man" (Ephesians 3:16). He then expresses his confidence several verses later that He "is able to do far more abundantly beyond all that we ask or think, according to the power that works within us" so that we're "filled up to all the fullness of God" (3:19-20). God's power forms our inner dimensions (thoughts, feelings, will, soul, bodily habits) so that they increasingly become like those of Jesus.

In Romans 7:14-23, Paul reveals how this works as a practical matter in our psychological life. Think about the steady fare of particular evils and goods that are part of our day-to-day experience whether we're on the giving or receiving end of them. Paul implies that those goods or evils come from inside others or us, which was a central teaching of Jesus. What we do on the outside comes from what we are on the inside. Paul's testimony in verses 14-23 unveils the inner conditions that produce the outer behavior, and I'm oversimplifying for the purpose of understanding. There are three of those.

In the first condition, we will to do a particular evil or not to do a particular good that is before us. Destructive thoughts, feelings, and/or bodily habits support or strengthen our will so that we do the evil or don't do the good.

In the second condition, the one Paul describes in verses 14-23, we will not to do the evil or to do the good. Destructive thoughts, feelings, and/or bodily habits though oppose and overcome our will so that we do the evil or don't do the good.

Finally, in the third condition, we will not to do the evil or to do the good. Constructive thoughts, feelings, and/or bodily habits then support or strengthen our will so that we don't do the evil or do the good.

The third condition, in totality, was that of Jesus. He always willed not to do the evil and to do the good before Him and constructive thoughts, feelings, and bodily habits always fully supported His will. Because they did, He never did the evil and always did the good. He was a psychologically and behaviorally perfect person.

We of course are not. We're born with a self-centered nature that's characterized by the first condition. But God's power regenerates us when we decide to become disciples of Jesus. It renews our heart so that we now routinely will not to do the evil or to do the good that is before us. The problem is that many thoughts, feelings, and bodily habits remain that oppose our regenerated will so that Paul's experience in 7:14-23 is ours as well. We do the evil we want not to do or don't do the good we want to do. But over the course of our lifetime as we faithfully carry out our discipleship to Jesus, God's power in us slowly but surely brings our thoughts, feelings, and bodily habits in line with our regenerated will. The supernatural result is that we increasingly don't do the evils and do the goods that present themselves to us in day-to-day life. Our psychological and behavioral life, what we are and do, becomes increasingly like the psychological and behavioral life of Jesus until the day we die.

The Bible and our own experiences in carrying out our discipleship to Jesus paint a practical and detailed picture of what this psychological and behavioral life looks like. We want to receive criticism graciously and learn from it and not to defensively criticize right back, and we do. We want to root for others to outshine us and not to envy them, and we do. We want to bless those who wrong us and not to retaliate, and we do. We want to honestly admit our fault when we're in the wrong and not to put a spin on it, and we do. That's increasingly our experience and it is because God's power works in us to transform what we are and do.

God unceasingly puts His power to work for us in a second way. The first way is that it works *in* us to transform what we are. The second is that it works *upon* us to enhance what we do. What we do refers to ministry. Ministry consists of three general activities directed to building God's kingdom on earth and meeting human needs: witnessing, giving money and possessions, and serving with our time, talents, and energy. That's ministry and God's power works upon us as we carry it out to increase its effectiveness.

Jesus was the quintessential model of empowered ministry. Acts 10:38 discloses that "God anointed Him with the Holy Spirit and power" so that "He went about doing good and healing all who were oppressed by the devil." Having veiled His divine attributes, He ministered in the power of God.

And so can we. Immediately preceding His ascension, He promised His first disciples that "you will receive power when the Holy Spirit has come upon you; and you shall be my witnesses." We learn from Colossians 1:10-11 that this promise is ours as well as theirs. Paul expresses his desire that the disciples at Colossae would "bear fruit in every good work . . . strengthened with all power, according to His glorious might." The world shattering result is that disciples of Jesus, collectively, are able to do "greater works" than He Himself did (John 14:12). Disciples being empowered to do those greater works is called "enhancement."

Enhancement manifests itself in two ways. One is in actions on our part that exceed the normal. We say and do things that are beyond our natural capacity to say and do. The other is in the effects of actions on our part that exceed the normal. The impact of what we say and do is beyond what would normally occur. In his *Merechristianthoughts Blog*, Fred Belcher quotes acclaimed missionary and apostle of world literacy Frank Laubach in that regard: "I feel simply carried along each hour, doing my part in a plan which is far beyond myself. This sense of cooperation with God in little things is what astonished me. I must work, to be sure, but there is God working along with me."[24] That's how God enhances ministry. He is right there working along with us, empowering either the nature or the effects of what we do.

A disciple of Jesus decided to confront her daughter about a sin in her life that was diminishing the lives of her children, the disciple's grandchildren. She prayed before she did that the Holy Spirit would empower her to speak with clarity, truth, and love and that He would inhabit her words so that her daughter would receive not reject them. She felt strangely confident the next day as she spoke to her daughter and found herself saying things that seemed to be beyond her own wisdom and understanding. Even so, she expected a backlash from her daughter who to her surprise listened attentively to what she said, began to cry, and asked for her help to overcome the habitual sin she faced. The disciple later commented that it was as if she wasn't speaking to her daughter, but as if God was speaking through her. She said things that were beyond her capacity to say and the effects were beyond what would normally occur. That's enhancement.

God's limitless power, as you can see, is something He can and does share with us. It works *in* us to transform us and *upon* us to enhance what we do for others and Him.

But it does so only if we position ourselves so it can. A central teaching of the Bible is that two worlds exist, the visible world of matter and the invisible world of God and His kingdom, which includes the powers of the age to come. In order to share in God's power, we must act upon and interact with the invisible world. Just as we act in specific ways to engage matter, we act in specific ways to engage God and His kingdom. I listed a sampling of those ways in Chapter 4: solitude and silence, fasting, study, prayer, lectio divina, practicing the presence, purposeful obedience, the musing of the mind upon Him, worship, thanksgiving, and conversation with Him. Practicing those activities or spiritual disciples as they're called positions us before God in such a way that He's able to put His power to work in us and for us.

It positions us in that way, however, only when it's done with vigor.

We must be brutally honest here and confess that among the majority of church going people it rarely is. Sociologist Tony Campolo makes a judicious observation about that in his book *Growing Up in America*: "The American religious mind on the whole is biased against spirituality. Americans aren't impressed with spiritual disciplines. We have nothing against them; it's just that we have more practical things to do."[25] His point is well taken. Most of us direct our minds and bodies with far more vitality to engaging the visible world than we do to engaging the invisible world.

A simple personal survey might be illuminating here. Do I spend as much time thinking about God as I do thinking about my spouse or children? Do I spend as much time fellowshipping with God as I do fellowshipping with people? Do I spend as much time reading the Bible as I do watching television? Do I spend as much time caring for my soul as I do caring for my possessions?

Make no mistake about it. You and I *can* share in the power of God. But we *will* only if the answers to those questions and others are "Yes." We must act upon and interact with the invisible world with at least the same intensity and focus that we do the visible world. We'll be powerful if we do because God is power full.

CHAPTER 9

"A KNOW-IT-ALL"

God Is Omniscient

A woman once confided in me that "My mother-in-law is a know-it-all." Regrettably, we all know from our own personal encounters what a know-it-all is. It's a person who talks and acts as if he or she knows everything about everything. In the literal not the idiomatic sense of the term, there are no know-it-alls, with one exception. That exception is God. He knows it all. He's omniscient.

God Is Omniscient Revealed

The Bible's most patent witness to the omniscience of God is 1 John 3:20. It asserts, "God knows all things." The Bible's descent into the details of those "all things" is mesmeric.

In Psalm 147:5, the psalmist states as tersely as John did that "His (God's) understanding is infinite." But one of the particulars He understands in verse 4 is gripping, "He counts the number of the stars; He gives names to them all." That He counts the number of the stars means that He knows every one that exists. That He gives names to them all means that He knows the nature of each. Astronomers estimate that there are approximately 10,000,000,000,000,000,000,000 stars in the universe, a number so large that we can't begin to wrap our minds around it. According to the psalmist, God knows everything there is to know about all of those stars.

The psalmist looks closer to our earthly home in Psalm 50:11. Quoting God, he writes, "I know every bird of the mountains, and everything that moves in the field is mine." Considering that there are 100 to 400 billion birds on earth, it's no small achievement that God knows everything there is to know about each one.

Jesus may be drawing on Psalm 50:11 when He pronounces in Matthew 10:29 that not one sparrow alights on the ground without Father God knowing it. He extends His pronouncement in verse 30 to the hairs on everyone's head. They're "all numbered" by Father God, implying that His omniscience is a critical factor in the personal care He gives us.

It isn't just the hairs of our head that God knows. David claims in Psalm 139:1-6 that it's everything else about us as well, including our thoughts (verses 2 and 4). Nobel Prize winner Daniel Kahneman poses the idea of a three second window that he calls the "psychological present." Assuming we have one thought every three seconds during the 16 hours a day that we're awake, that's 20,000 thoughts a day. David proclaims with confidence that God knows each one.

The texts I've cited are sufficient to elicit from us Paul's response in Romans 11:33. It's a paean of praise to God's omniscience: "Oh, the depth of the riches both of the wisdom and knowledge of God! How unsearchable are His judgments and unfathomable His ways!" Notice the exclamation marks. They're appropriate. As much as any other attribute of His, the omniscience of God makes us want to fall on our face before Him and cry "Glory!"

God Is Omniscient Explained

The word "omniscient" is derived from the Latin roots *omnis* denoting "all" and *scientia* denoting "knowledge." That God is omniscient means that He has all knowledge. His knowledge is limitless. Or as 1 John 3:20 says it, He "knows all things." More precisely, He knows everything there is to know about everything. He knows everything that can possibly be known whether it's actual or potential. He always has and He always will.

It necessarily follows that His knowledge had no beginning.

Identify something you know and when and how you came to know it. I know, for example, that washing white clothes with dark clothes makes the white clothes dingy. Ignorantly washing whites with darks in college and observing their change in appearance taught me that. Or I know interested people do whatever is convenient and committed people do whatever is necessary. Ken Blanchard taught me that in his book *The One Minute Manager*. Thinking about everything you and I know, it's obvious we at one time didn't know it and we know it now because a person or an experience taught it to us.

God, in contrast, has never *not known* something or has never *come to know* something. People receive Bachelor's Degrees, Masters Degrees, and Ph.D. Degrees and we say they're "highly educated." He in contrast isn't educated at all and doesn't need to be. No person or event has ever taught Him anything and never will. He never comes to know something He didn't know because He has always known everything there is to know. His knowledge had no beginning because He's omniscient.

For the same reason, His knowledge has no end.

We can't say the same about us can we? According to a 2013 study commissioned by "Post-It" notes maker 3M, the average person forgets four facts, items, or events every day. That's 1,460 every year.[26] All of us can point to facts or truths, whether vital or trivial, that we at one time knew but now don't. Forgetting is an inevitable part of our cognitive experience.

It isn't part of God's. What He knows now, which is everything, He'll always know. He literally never forgets anything He knows no matter how serious or slight. Some maintain that there's at least one exception in Hebrews 8:12 and the Old Testament text it quotes, Isaiah 43:25, in which God says,

"For I will be merciful to their iniquities, and I will remember their sins no more." One long standing Christian referenced those texts and concluded from them: "Did you know that I can do something that God can't do? I can remember my sins, while God cannot." It might be a comforting thought but it's also self-deceiving. The psalmist and the author of Hebrews employ figurative language here, hyperbole, to communicate the vigor of God's forgiveness. He regards and treats us as if we hadn't committed the sins He's forgiven, but He never forgets them because, despite the claims of open theists, He can't. Just as His knowledge can have no beginning because He's omniscient, it can also have no end.

His never beginning and never ending knowledge reaches beyond the actual to the potential. He knows what *will be* real or true (the potential) as surely as He knows what *has been* and *is* real or true (the actual). So, the 46th president of the United States is as much a part of His knowledge as the current 45th, Donald Trump. Or the day of our death is as much a part of His knowledge as the day of our birth. He knows what *will be* as fully as He knows what *has been* and *is*. Consequently, He's never "caught off guard" as we say it and never unprepared. The psalmist expresses God's current knowledge of the potential and personalizes it as well in Psalm 139:4, "Even before there is a word on my tongue, Behold, O LORD, You know it all." I wonder, "What is the last word you will speak before you die." God doesn't wonder about that or anything else that's potential. He knows.

I stumbled across an enjoyable website, *did-you-knows.com*. Did you know the following: "the average person laughs ten times a day," "the average bed contains over 6 billion dust mites," "the average life span of a mosquito is two weeks," the average person swallows 295 times during a meal," "the average cow produces 40 glasses of milk a day," and "the average person shed 1.5 pounds of skin each year."[27] God has always known all of those things and all things, knows them now, and will always know them. He's omniscient. He literally knows it all.

God Is Omniscient Applied

And He reveals some of what He knows to us. That He does addresses an issue of great concern in our cultural context. What does it mean to be educated? Google the question and the attention and space it's given will likely surprise you.

Several years ago, I filled out an application form that asked, "What is your education?" Knowing the information that was being sought, I answered "Bachelors Degree, Masters Degree, and J.D. Degree" and was right in doing so. But does having ten years of higher education and three degrees make me educated? At a Harvard graduation ceremony years ago, President James Bryan Conant welcomed the graduates into "the Fellowship of Educated Men." His comment reflects the thinking of typical Americans then and now. To be educated means to earn a degree from an institution of higher learning. One who has a degree, they conclude, is educated; one who doesn't isn't.

But is that what it means to be educated and uneducated? In his influential book *The Presentation of Self in Everyday Life*, sociological theorist Irving Goffman contends that the idea that having degrees makes people educated and competent to serve is a con job. He asks the hard-headed question, "Does it really take ten years to train a doctor, six years to train a lawyer or seven years to train a member of the clergy, or are these years in higher education part of the con job?"[28] In my view, it doesn't. We're being conned to believe that those who earn a degree from a college or university are educated and that those who don't aren't. It's a con because both propositions are false. The truth is that many of you who don't have degrees from colleges or universities are highly educated and that some of you who have degrees aren't.

Let me quickly clear the air. I'm not a crank who denigrates the significance of a higher education. We most certainly want those who design our buildings, perform our surgeries, represent our cases in court, and so on to be formally trained. It enables them to add great value to our lives by doing what they do. But it doesn't make them or anyone else educated in the truest sense of the word.

What does? Good sense tells us. It's knowing "the best information possible on the most important matters."[29] The most important matters are those that most impact us and preoccupy our attention and action because they do. They include death, life after death, money, sex, power, marriage, raising children, lawsuits, love, anger, words, influencing people for good, rivalry, the human body, the psychology of the self, dress, laziness, forgiveness, overcoming evil, work, and criticism to name a few. Anyone who knows the best information about those and other most important matters is truly educated. Anyone who doesn't know it isn't.

It's here that God's omniscience comes into play. Since He's omniscient, He knows everything there is to know about every subject or concern that absorbs us in our day-to-day lives. And He reveals some of what He knows to us in the Bible, which He wrote through its authors. Since He loves us and wants us to thrive, what He reveals in the Bible is the best information about the most important matters in human life.

Examples abound. 1 Corinthians 6:16 teaches us that to touch a person's body in sex is to touch his or her soul so that there's no such thing as "casual sex." Or Matthew 7:1-12 teaches us that the best way to influence people for good is not to condemn or force but to ask in the context of goodness. Or Ephesians 6:5-8 and Colossians 3:22-25 teach us that there is glory in every job (however much or little humans esteem it) and how to find it. That sampling of texts demonstrates what the Bible gives us. It's the best information about the most important matters in human life.

The consequence is sweeping. A physician who doesn't know what God reveals about the human body in the Bible is insufficiently educated. An attorney who doesn't know what God reveals about lawsuits in the Bible is insufficiently educated. A marriage counselor who doesn't know what God reveals about marriage in the Bible is insufficiently educated. Those who have multiple degrees from institutions of higher learning but don't know the Bible aren't as educated as they need to be.

On the other hand, those who have no degrees from institutions of higher learning but have a working knowledge of what God reveals in the Bible are truly educated. I'm acquainted with individuals who have no formal training beyond high school. But they know the Bible through and through, which makes them some of the best educated individuals I know.

Our calling, in the face of that, is crystal clear. Firmly make and devotedly carry out the decision to gain a working knowledge of the Bible. To have a working knowledge of the Bible means to understand in detail the meaning and application of its contents. Ephesians 5:22-33 illustrates what I mean. In this text, the God who knows it all gives the best information about the most important matter of marriage. He states, for instance, that a husband should love his wife as he does his own body. It's an incisive psychological and relational insight, the meaning and application of which we must seek to understand, and without which we cannot know what we need to know about marriage. It's imperative that we make and carry out the decision to gain a strong working knowledge of the Bible.

We carry out that decision by studying not just reading it. First, we learn the principles for interpreting it, what academics call "hermeneutics." Second, we then apply those principles with concentration and good sense to the text before us. Our intention is to understand the meaning and application of as many Biblical texts as we can in our lifetimes. We then become increasingly educated as we carry out our intention.

That isn't to insinuate that you and I will ever know it all because we won't. But we can know most of what the God who does know it all reveals to us. We're truly educated when we do.

CHAPTER 10

"FATHER KNOWS BEST"

God Is All-Wise

One of the hit sitcoms of the 1950's was *Father Knows Best*. Robert Young starred as a wise family man who as weekly episodes sometimes showed, wasn't always so wise. Despite the sitcom's title, he didn't always know what was best. But there is One who does. That One is God. God always knows what's best because He's all-wise.

God Is All-Wise Revealed

The Bible is unfaltering in its testimony of God's wisdom.

Proverbs 8:22 personifies wisdom and presents it as saying, "The LORD possessed me at the beginning of His way before His works of old." God possessed wisdom before anything else but He existed.

What Proverbs 8:22 implies, Psalm 104:24 states. God's wisdom actively directed His creation of the universe: "O LORD, how many are Your works! In wisdom You have made them all." The universe and every aspect of it reflect the wealth of God's wisdom.

Daniel 2:19-23 digs deeper by linking God's wisdom and power with His name or nature, verse 20. It teaches us by doing so that wisdom is an essence of God's nature. He is as wise as He is powerful. Verses 21 and 23 add the further insight that He is as a result the source of all other wisdom. Anyone else who has it, angelic or human, got it from Him.

A stronger statement still is found in Romans 16:27. Paul is resolute in affirming that God is "the only wise God." The words "only wise" indicate that He is wise in Himself and that all other wisdom, angelic or human, is a pale reflection of His.

In my view, Colossians 2:3 is the most vibrant assertion of God's wisdom. Paul writes about Jesus "in whom are hidden all the treasures of wisdom and knowledge." The words "all the treasures of" connote "the sum total of." The sum total of wisdom resides in Jesus. Based on what we learned about the Trinity, that necessarily means that the sum total of wisdom resides in the Father and Holy Spirit as well.

God Is All-Wise Explained

God's wisdom is logically and functionally linked with His knowledge. Some in fact define wisdom as the right use of knowledge. That definition, while inadequate, does show that God's wisdom and knowledge are partners. They go together. His knowledge is always at work in His wisdom and His wisdom in His knowledge.

His wisdom is of the same character as His knowledge and every other attribute of His. First, it's infinite. It's limitless or measureless. He isn't just wise. He's all-wise. Second, it's perfect. In the Bible, wisdom has a moral as well as a cognitive component. That it does is a central tenet of the Book of Proverbs. It's more than intelligence and knowledge on the one hand and cleverness and cunning on the other. It's those things harnessed to objectives or ends that are good and right. That moral component, along with the cognitive, is fully manifested in God's wisdom so that its perfection matches its infinity.

To appreciate the grandness of this infinite and perfect wisdom of His, we must ascertain its nuances with some precision. We'd do well to turn to theologian J.I. Packer here whose version of wisdom is as precise as it is practical: "Wisdom is the power to see, and the inclination to choose, the best and highest goal, together with the surest means of attaining it."[30] We're able to discern the three nuances of wisdom in Packer's words. First, it sees the greatest good in whatever the situation is before it. Second, it sees the best means for achieving that greatest good. And third, it employs those best means effectively to achieve the greatest good. Simply put, wisdom knows best. It knows what is best, knows the best way to pursue what is best, and pursues it with competence that way.

God is infinitely and perfectly wise in just that sense. First, He always knows what is best in every possible situation. What is best is primarily His own glory and secondarily the greatest good for the most people. Second, He always knows the best way to pursue what is best. He recognizes the means that are most effective for accomplishing it. And third, He always pursues what is best in the best way. With utter competence, He employs the means in the ways that are the most effective in accomplishing it.

That's God's wisdom and in conjunction with His limitless power, we rejoice in it don't we? Think about it. Power without wisdom is frightening. Some years ago, Jim Carrey starred in a movie titled *Bruce Almighty* that is theologically bankrupt on many levels. One is that God gives Carrey's character all of His power but none of His wisdom and assigns him the business of running life on earth, whereupon he quickly finds out how dangerous power without wisdom is. He begins answering people's prayers, for instance, but doesn't know what is best. In desperation, he just gives everyone everything they ask for, which soon causes chaos in their lives in particular and human life in general. He learns the hard way that limitless power without limitless wisdom is perilous beyond imagination.

But in God, limitless power and limitless wisdom are united, making Him capable of running the universe and the individual lives of the humans who inhabit it with absolute mastery. His wisdom is always active and never fails. He never has to say "oops" because He never makes a mistake in what He decides and does. His wisdom is flawless.

The word "flawless" deserves elaboration. In his book *Good to Great*, Jim Collins promulgates his thesis that people tend to settle for the good instead of pursuing the great thereby making the good the enemy of the great. The word "best" can be substituted for the word "great" without changing Collin's thesis. Good is the enemy of best. But there is no rivalry between the two in God. We all know that He never decides and does what is bad. But in a similar vein, He never decides and does what is good. He wouldn't be infinitely and perfectly wise if He did. God knows what He's doing. He always decides and does what is best and nothing less.

God Is All-Wise Applied

The practical relevance of God's wisdom to us resides in Jesus' striking observation in John 6:63, "the words that I have spoken to you are spirit and life." The chorus of an old hymn, *Wonderful Words of Life*, echoes the observation of Jesus. It rightly describes the words of the Father, Son, and Holy Spirit as "beautiful words, wonderful words, wonderful words of life." The beauty and wonder of God's words spring from His wisdom that knows best. They substantially link us with real life by revealing the best way to live it out in its details.

Many if not most of God's professed followers don't believe that. Their comments when they hear His words and their responses after they do betray what they do believe instead.

I once counseled bitter Christian grandparents who had a wicked daughter-in-law. She wanted her out of town parents and not them to be the "'A' grandparents" and so, rarely let them see their grandchildren. She also poisoned their grandchildren's minds, saying bad things about them that were untrue. They came to me, explained the situation, and asked my advice. I answered by quoting God's words in Romans 12:21, "Overcome evil with good." I told them to start with that guiding principle and then descend into the details of it as it applied to their situation. I'll never forget the grandmother's incredulous reply, with which the grandfather agreed, "Get real!" They then left my office with no intention at all of overcoming evil with good.

Their reply, "Get real," implied what they and a sizeable cross-section of professing Christians take God's words to be. They're dogma and/or law.[31] Dogma is something we think we have to believe even if we actually doubt it. Law is something we think we have to do even if it's bad for us. I say "have to" believe or do it because we think God will punish us if we don't.

Dogma and law have a common thread. Both view God's words as arbitrary and unrelated to real life. They simply don't work. They make day-to-day life difficult, sometimes even dangerous, but He requires us to believe or do them anyway. That thinking lay behind the "get real" response of the grandparents and if my pastoral counseling experiences are any indication, it's typical. The idea that "this circumstance will get worse not better if I do what God says" is characteristic of professing Christians. His words are dogma or law.

But having learned about God's perfect and limitless wisdom, we know better. His words always reveal what is best. We don't take them to be something we have to believe and do because He'll punish us if we don't. Quite the opposite, we take them to be something so beneficial to us that we'd be fools to disregard them. We're enthusiasts when it comes to them. We eagerly do two things.

First, we "hang on" all of God's words as we say it.

That's what we do isn't it when we consider words to be reality and vital information. We hang on them. After my wife Jill's colon cancer surgery, we kept an appointment with her oncologist. We believed something as he was speaking to us. It's that he knew best about cancer and that his words were reality and vital information to us. So, we hung on every one. We listened intently to everything he said in order to understand it.

It's the same with God. He knows best about life, which makes his words absolute reality and the most vital of all information to us. So, we hang on every one. We listen intently to everything He says in order to understand it. We do that practically by carefully interpreting as many of the words, sentences, and verses in the Bible as we can before we die.

Believing God knows best, we eagerly do a second thing. We don't just hang on all of His words. We live them out as well.

Or do we? I've concluded from years of listening to professing Christians and observing them that many of us sometimes don't. I recall the words of an indignant Christian mother whose fourth grade daughter was wronged by her teacher: "I know we're supposed to forgive and I will if you hurt me. But don't you dare hurt my children." She didn't forgive the teacher but it wasn't because she tried and failed. It was because she didn't intend to. Some of God's words, we think, are too foolish to live out. They're so unrealistic that we can't live them out. Or they're so prejudicial that others or we will be harmed if we do. So, we don't.

The reality of course is quite different. God's words are utter wisdom and thus, we live them out. Because Jill and I believed that her oncologist knew what was best, we not only hung on his every word but left his office and did everything he told us to do. The understanding and belief that God is all-wise and knows what's best leads to that very same end. Root for our competitors to outshine us and rejoice when they do. Bless those who wrong us. Care for the needs of those who sue us. Receive criticism not give it back. Live simply not extravagantly. If we confidently believe it's most beneficial for others and us to do those things and all things God says, we'll try and train our best to do them.

Jesus has the last word on the subject in His conclusion to the Sermon on the Mount. It's His heralded parable of the two foundations in Matthew 7:24-27: "Everyone who hears these words of Mine and acts on them, may be compared to a wise man who built his house on the rock . . . Everyone who hears these words of Mine and does not act on them, will be like a foolish man who build his house on the sand." We're wise if we hang on God's words and live them out. We're foolish if we don't. Why? It's because Father (and Son and Holy Spirit) knows best.

CHAPTER 11

"HOW CAN I BE SURE?"

God Is Immutable

"How can I be sure? In a world that's constantly changing, how can I be sure where I stand with you?"[32] That's the question the Young Rascals asked in their 1967 hit song by that name and it's a pressing one. We desperately want to be sure of where we stand with people but we can't because they change. In contrast, we can be sure of where we stand with God because He doesn't change. He's immutable.

God Is Immutable Revealed

The Bible's testimony of God's immutability isn't as wide-ranging as that of His other attributes but it needn't be. If only one verse states a proposition, that proposition is as much truth as one that a hundred verses state. In that sense, God's immutability is as well-established as His love, holiness, or any other divine attribute is.

At the end of his rope in Psalm 102, the psalmist divulges the source of his confidence that God will end his suffering and prolong his life. It's that "You (God) are the same, and Your years will not come to an end" (verse 27). He desires and intends to pursue the psalmist's well-being and since He's always the same, always will.

God Himself speaks of His immutability in Malachi 3:6. He impresses upon the post-exilic Israelites how advantageous this attribute of His is to them, "I, the LORD, do not change; therefore you, O sons of Jacob, are not consumed." He comforts them with the thought that He was gracious to their forefathers and because He doesn't change is just as gracious to them.

Jesus' little brother James uses a creative metaphor to articulate God's immutability in 1:17 of his New Testament letter, "Every good thing given and every perfect gift is from above, coming down from the Father of lights, with whom there is no variation or shifting shadow." The best gifts that humans enjoy come from God who is the Father of heavenly lights, including the sun. The "shifting shadow" refers to the sun from our perspective. We experience its light and heat on earth in varying degrees depending on the time of day and its position in relation to us. It feels hotter and seems brighter to us during the middle of the day than it does at the beginning and the end of it, after which, during the night, we don't feel or see it at all. Our experience of God doesn't have to be like that, James teaches us here. It can be consistent because He never varies from what He is.

The Biblical record is unmistakable in its declaration of God's immutability.

God Is Immutable Explained

This attribute of His is especially germane in the framework of our ever-changing world. Solomon bespeaks our lot in life in his familiar "A Time for Everything" text, Ecclesiastes 3:1-8. Derek Kidner's creative commentary on this text captures the gist of it.[33] We dance to many tunes not of our own making and nothing we experience or pursue has any permanence. Our masters are the calendar and the tide of events that repeatedly move us from one circumstance now to its opposite later. Life's reversals and sudden shifts make the circumstances that are before us transient and subject to constant change. The things that are most important to us – relationships, health, jobs, the stock market, the weather, the seasons, personal finances, technologies, and neighborhoods to name a few – have this in common. Variation and shift, for better or worse, are woven into the very fabric of what they are. Things change.

God, however, doesn't. He's immutable. The Westminster Shorter Catechism asks, "What is God?" It answers, "God is a Spirit, infinite, eternal, and *unchangeable, in his being*." That God is immutable means that He's unchangeable in His being. His nature never changes. Sameness is woven into the very fabric of what He is.

The nature of a being can change in one of two ways. One way is quantitatively. It can increase by acquiring attributes it doesn't possess or it can decrease by losing attributes it does. The other way is qualitatively. It can improve by attributes it possesses maturing or it can worsen by attributes it possesses degenerating.

But because God is limitless and perfect, He has never experienced either of those changes and never will. He has always possessed all of the positive attributes that it's possible for a being to possess and always will. He has likewise never possessed any of the negative attributes that it's possible for a being to possess and never will. Consequently, He has not ever acquired or lost any attributes and never will. Also, all the attributes He possesses have always been fully developed and complete and always will be. None of his attributes, therefore, has ever improved or worsened and never will.

The idea is widely held that "the God of the Old Testament is not the God of the New Testament." God is vengeful and wrathful in the Old Testament and gracious and loving in the New, as if He somehow matured and grew. It's a false idea that His immutability debunks. God is the same now as He was in the Old Testament, a God of perfect and limitless love, grace, holiness, and wrath.

He is because no change, either positive or negative, is possible in Him. Alluding to Hebrews 13:8, He is exactly *the same* in all His attributes "yesterday and today and forever." The bottom line is this. As He has always been, He is now, and as He is now, He will always be, down to the smallest detail of any attribute of His. No change of any kind is possible in Him. He is in His nature devoid of change.

God Is Immutable Applied

In view of His sovereignty over our world and us, we can breathe a sigh of relief that He is.

19th century Scottish historian and philosopher Thomas Carlyle popularized the "Great Man Theory" of history. This theory argues that history is best explained with reference to the gifted individuals who shape it. Carlyle held that "Great men should rule and that others should revere them." The masses, he believed, should make great men dictators, entrusting them with absolute power to rule as they willed.

We ourselves might endorse a dictatorship as the most beneficial and efficient form of government but only under two conditions. One is that the dictator is truly a great man. He's possessed of character that compels him to do what is good and right and competence that enables him to do it. The other condition is that he must always remain great. A great man can be entrusted with absolute power only if it's certain that his character and competence are constant and will never change. Unless those two conditions are met, it's dangerous to surrender ourselves to a dictator.

The fly in the ointment is that the second of those conditions can't be met. If there's anything history teaches us, it's that dictators and rulers often change not for the better but for the worse. Lord Acton's famous maxim, "Power tends to corrupt, and absolute power corrupts absolutely" acknowledges this. It's a legitimate concern of ours that the great man who rules beneficently and capably now may become less than a great man who rules malevolently or ineptly later.

What is a legitimate concern with regard to human rulers is no concern at all with regard to our divine ruler. God's limitless presence, knowledge, and power as Creator enable Him to be what He is – the absolute sovereign or ruler over our world. He is to our world what an absolute dictator is to his nation. He totally controls it. As the old spiritual says it, He has the whole world in His hands. And we can be glad that He does because He's utterly good and great. But what if He changed and became less good or great? It's a disconcerting thought but we needn't entertain it because He can't change and won't. He'll always reign over our world with the same perfect and limitless character (goodness) and competence (greatness) that He does now. We can always be sure of His beneficent posture toward our world because He's immutable.

The relevance of God's immutability, however, extends beyond His relation to the world generally to His relation to you and me individually. Because He's changeless, we can be just as sure of His posture toward us as we're sure of His posture toward it.

What marks our relationship with God, certainty, is absent in our relationships with humans because they, unlike Him, change. Their nature (the condition of their inner dimensions) is always forming. Our capacity to change and transform is perhaps the most distinguishing feature of humans. The upshot of this ongoing formation is that every individual with whom we have a relationship is a different person now than he or she was, and will be a different person than he or she is now.

The inconstancy of human nature infuses our human relationships with an air of uncertainty and doubt and we easily discern why it does. Since people's posture toward us is rooted in their nature, which changes, their posture toward us may change as well. We can never be sure of where we stand with them as a result. A wife remarked that she was married once to five different men, indicating her frustration with her one husband's changing nature and the unpredictability in their marriage that it created. It's a hard pill to swallow but swallow it we must. The people with whom we have relationships are continually morphing so that their postures toward us often are as well, either for good or ill. What if it's for ill? It answers the comment of several abandoned wives, "I never dreamed when I married that my husband would do such a thing." The answer is that their husbands were not the kind of person when they married who would do such a thing. But they formed into the kind of person who would. There's no doubting it. Because humans change, we can never be 100% sure of where we stand or will stand with them.

Though they shouldn't, many project this reality of relationship with people on to their relationship with God. Pagan religions worship temperamental gods that regard and treat them according to whatever their whims may be at the moment. The one true God of course isn't like that but many think and act as if He is. One of the poignant moments of my ministry occurred when a woman stricken with cancer blurted out, "Why does God hate me?" She went to on explain what she meant. She must have done something horribly wrong for God to punish her with cancer. Note her unspoken assumption that human actions can change God's posture of love toward us to a posture of hate.

They cannot because God is immutable. That necessarily means his posture toward us is unaffected by anything that occurs outside of Him including human actions. There's nothing temperamental at all about Him so that His posture toward us is always the same. He regards and treats us with perfect and limitless love, goodness, holiness, and justness now and because His nature never changes always will no matter what. His thinking and acting in relation to us will never be more or less loving, good, holy, and just than it is now.

Living with confidence and joy in a world driven by change requires that we live with the certainty that understands and believes that. Confidence and joy are psychologically impossible without certainty.

Some counterpoise that a degree of uncertainty in relationships is beneficial in that it's an antidote to carelessness and neglect. If a guy becomes too sure of his girl, for instance, he might treat her less than he should. Or if a girl thinks she has her guy "in the bag," she might start taking him for granted. In contrast, doubt about where the guy stands with the girl or the girl with the guy spurs the attentiveness of the one to the other.

Those same dynamics, some argue, partially explain the hiddenness of God. His concealment of Himself from us cultivates uncertainty in our relationship with Him, which "keeps us on our toes." It causes us to be more careful and vigilant in our actions upon Him and for Him.

That point of view contains a kernel of truth but in the end, the disadvantages of uncertainty in our relationship with God outweigh any of its advantages. The famed 19th century Danish philosopher Soren Kierkegaard was a classic case in point. He constantly fretted over the disturbing question of whether or not God was going to finally condemn him. This doubt of his plagued the entirety of his life, making him an unhappy man who people called "the gloomy Dane." Kierkegaard of all people was living breathing proof that uncertainty and doubt about God's posture toward us tortures us spiritually and psychologically, arresting our confidence and joy.

The immutability of God drives the clouds of uncertainty and doubt away. Meditate on three texts that delineate where we stand with God if we're disciples of Jesus. In Psalm 56:9, David asserts, "This I know, that God is for me." The author of Psalm 118 possessed the same conviction, declaring in verse 6, "The LORD is for me; I will not fear." Paul concurred with both psalmists contending about all disciples of Jesus and him in Romans 8:31, "If God is for us, who is against us." It can't be stated any more plainly than that. God is for us. He's in our corner.

The psalmist's declaration in Psalm 118:6, "I will not fear" and Paul's rhetorical question in Romans 8:31, "Who is against us?" reveal how He being for us plays out in real life. We are beyond irreversible harm in this life (Romans 8:28) and any harm at all in the life to come (Revelation 21:4) and are within the purview of His constant blessing of us (Ephesians 1:3). That's where we stand with God now and because He's immutable, we always will.

Thoroughly understanding and truly believing that is what Paul calls in Philippians 4:12 "the secret of being filled and going hungry, both of having abundance and suffering need." When we know in our mind of minds and heart of hearts that God is for us and will always be, the overriding tone of confidence and joy that pervaded Paul's day-to-day life through thick and thin will pervade ours as well.

With that stirring thought in mind, we're ready to finalize our answer to the question the Young Rascals asked, only taken a step further, "In a world that's constantly changing, how can I be sure where I stand with God?" We can be sure because He's immutable. He never changes and neither does His posture toward us. He's "for us" now and forever.

CHAPTER 12

"THIS I KNOW"

God Is Love

If I asked you to fill in the blank "God is," what would your answer be? God has an attribute for which He is almost universally known. I've learned from conversations over the years that even the most secular or Biblically illiterate people, who know almost nothing about the Christian faith or even God Himself, usually know this attribute of His. It's so well known in fact that people, including Christians, tend to associate Him almost exclusively with it. You yourself undoubtedly know of what I write. It's that God is love.

God Is Love Revealed

The Bible drips with the love of God. It's stated explicitly and implicitly and narrated more than any other attribute of His save one.

Before writing the Ten Commandments on tablets for the second time, God announces to Moses in Exodus 34:6-7 that He is "The LORD. The LORD God, compassionate and gracious, slow to anger, and abounding in lovingkindness and truth." Those are weighty words and Bible commentator Alan Cole spells out why, "Here is God, in Self-revelation, proclaiming His very Self to Moses."[34] God is in His "very Self" overflowing with compassion, grace, and love.

In a remarkable commentary on His choosing of Israel over the other nations, God clarifies the "Why?" behind His love in Deuteronomy 7:7-8, "The LORD did not set His love on you nor choose you because you were more in number than any of the peoples, for you were the fewest of all peoples, but because the LORD loved you." He didn't love the Israelites because they were greater numerically, culturally, economically, or militarily than other people groups. A simple paraphrase of His affirmation is, "I love you because I love you," an insight into His being that the New Testament extends to us all. It means He loves us not because we are what we are but because He is what He is.

1 John 4:8, 16 reveals what He is. Verses 8 and 16 contain what one commentator calls a "statement of God's substance." There are four such statements in the New Testament, each of which contains a subject, "God", a linking verb, "is," and a predicate adjective that tells us something about the subject, "God." They are as follows: (1) "God is *spirit*" (John 4:24); (2) "God is *a consuming fire*" (Hebrews 12:29); (3) "God is *light*" (1 John 1:5); and (4) "God is *love*" (1 John 4:8, 16). That fourth statement of God's substance is the most widely known proposition about Him and explains Deuteronomy 7:7-8. God loves us because of what He is, love.

The Bible spells out the range of God's love in spatial terms. David writes about it in Psalm 103:11 that "as high as the heavens are above the earth, so great is His lovingkindness toward those who fear Him." Paul enlarges on David's simile in Ephesians 3:18-19 by expressing his desire that his readers "may be able to comprehend with all the saints what is the breadth and length and height and depth, and to know the love of Christ which surpasses knowledge." The quality and extent of God's love for us is limitless and it's beyond us because it is.

The best we can do to understand it is to stack it up against what we consider the most heartfelt of all human loves, that of a mother for her nursing child. God Himself does just that in an eye catching text that He directs to Israel and by extension to us, Isaiah 49:15. God asks the rhetorical question, "Can a woman forget her nursing child and have no compassion on the son of her womb?" The implied answer, absent the mental illness or moral perversity of the mother, is "No." The woman bore the child and her own body sustains its life, generating within her an impulse of affection and care that's unexcelled in human relationships. Yet, the mother's bearing toward her nursing child doesn't even approach God's for us. As He states in the next line in verse 15, "Even these may forget, but I will not forget you." A mother's warmth and concern for her nursing child doesn't even approach God's for us. Isaiah 49:15 is, I believe, the strongest expression of God's love for us in the Bible.

King Solomon, in a candid moment, confessed what he knew and didn't know in Ecclesiastes 9:1: "For I have taken all of this to my heart and explain it that righteous men, wise men, and their deeds are in the hand of God. Man does not know whether it will be love or hatred anything awaits him." Creation, he opines, shows a glorious and powerful creator but not, with its mixed bag of good and bad, how He's disposed toward us. We can't deduce from it whether He hates us or loves us. That's true but creation isn't the only or even the best revelator. The Bible is, and as our small sampling of texts make crystal clear, a prime thread of truth runs through it from beginning to end. God loves us without limit, or as John says it, He "is love."

God Is Love Explained

And almost everyone knows it. I once counseled a middle-aged woman, a third generation non-Christian, who was so unacquainted with Christianity that she didn't know the Bible contained chapter and verse divisions. But when I asked her what she knew about God, she quickly answered, "He is love." That He is love is the most widely known proposition about Him.

It's also the most widely misunderstood. A quick grammar review from our grade school days unfolds the interpretive issue regarding it. A simple sentence has a subject, linking verb, and a predicate. The predicate can be a nominative telling us what the subject is or an adjective telling us something about the subject. Therein lays the issue. Is the word "love" in the simple sentence "God is love" a predicate nominative or a predicate adjective?

A bit of simple reasoning yields the answer. If it's a predicate nominative, the sentence means that love is what God is or to say it another way, God=love. It's on the same plane of reality that He is. But because God has no equals or opposites (Chapter 2), we can conclude that the word "love" is a predicate adjective. It tells us something about Him not what He is. Love isn't Him. It's only something that is true about Him. The sentence "God is love" doesn't equate Him with love; it identifies love as an attribute of His.

It's here that countless people make a fatal mistake. They equate God with love. Love is His essential nature, they believe, that consumes every other attribute of His, including His holiness. Presuming that He acts only in His love, they count on Him blessing them not harming them no matter how they live.

Therein lays their confidence, but it's a confidence misplaced. Love tells us something about God, not what He is. His other attributes aren't consumed in it. He always acts in all of His attributes together. His love does find expression in everything He does but so do all of His other attributes. Whenever He acts in His love, for instance, He also acts in His holiness, or whenever He acts in His holiness, He also acts in His love. He never suspends His other attributes to exercise His love. They all work equally, perfectly, and harmoniously together all the time, which reveals the delusion under which many people operate. They cannot count on

Him blessing them not harming them no matter how they live. His holiness is as operative in His response to evildoers as His love is.

While God isn't only love, He is love, and it's the one attribute of His, perhaps more than any other, that draws us to Him. Knowing it by description and acquaintance is the apex of human experience both now in this life and forever in the life to come. If we had every other positive experience possible to its fullest possible extent, except His love, life would be empty now and forever. Two aspects of it are particularly enthralling so that they deserve our attention and thought.

One is its source. Notice that John doesn't say that God is "loving" but that God is "love." That way of stating it implies what its source is. It's His nature. Recalling Deuteronomy 7:7-8, the cause of His love isn't anything in the ones He loves. It doesn't proceed from some quality or qualities in them such as intelligence, goodness, beauty, talent, influence, wealth, and more. It proceeds from some quality in Him, His love. He doesn't love them because *they are* lovely and lovable. He loves them because *He is* love. The source of His love is Him.

It's a remarkable reality that has three life altering ramifications.

First, God loves everyone indiscriminately. A website published a list of the top ten most hated people in history that included Adolph Hitler and Joseph Stalin. God, unlike most humans, loved them because He never considers whether or not a person is worthy of being loved. Worth has nothing to do with it. It's in His nature to love without partiality and He does so. Some estimate that 110 billion persons have lived in history. He loves every one of those 110 billion persons who has lived and will love every person who will ever live. There has never been a person He has not loved and there will never be a person He won't love.

Second, God loves everyone equally. Since He is in His nature perfect and limitless, He loves every person the same, that is, as much as it's possible for a person to be loved. So,

He loves the mentally challenged 10 year-old I met as much as the 12 year-old genius I read about who's entering college. Or He loves every radicalized terrorist as much as He does the most devoted disciple of Jesus. He has not, does not, and never will love one person even slightly more or less than another.

Third, God loves everyone unfailingly. He never stops loving anyone as much as it's possible to be loved despite what he or she becomes or does. There isn't anything a person can become or do that diminishes or destroys God's love for him or her. He loved Adolph Hitler and Joseph Stalin when they died just as He did when they were born. His love is unaffected by how unlovely or unlovable a person becomes. He has never stopped loving anyone and has never loved anyone less than He did and He never will.

God's indiscriminate, equal, and unfailing love alters our spiritual and psychological lives if we personalize it by applying it to us. First, He loves me as He does everyone. Second, He loves me as much He has ever loved anyone and ever will love anyone. And third, nothing I become or do will diminish or destroy His limitless love for me. What joy producing, relationship sealing, and hope generating realities those are and it's all because His love is rooted in Him not us.

There's a second aspect of God's love that deserves our attention and thought. The first is its source. The second is its nature, which has three aspects.

One is what psychologists call emotional identification. God feels what we feel. God does possess an attribute called impassibility. He doesn't involuntarily suffer or experience passions as a consequence of what we experience or do or what happens to us. He does empathize and experiences something like emotions but empathy and emotions don't come upon Him as they do us. They're willed by Him not forced upon Him by something outside of him. He isn't controlled by them as humans are but controls them. He must will to feel in other words and He does. He wills to feel what we feel.

Parental love, by way of analogy, gives us at least an inkling of what He experiences in relation to us. It's said that a child is a parent's heart walking around outside of him or her and that most parents are only as happy as their unhappiest child. Those two experiences of parents constitute emotional identification. Their hearts are inseparably bound to their children's happiness until the day they die. God has that same kind of experience in relation to us. Speaking figuratively of course, He has voluntarily bound up His heart with our happiness. He's chooses to feel what we feel and does. Using Paul's language in Romans 12:15 and applying it to God, He chooses to rejoice when we rejoice and weep when we weep. Think of the happiest and saddest moments in your life. God was there sharing your happiness and sadness with you. He identifies emotionally with us.

A second aspect of God's love is attention.

A lifelong single woman in her 60's was having dinner with a friend when she received a cell phone call from the man with whom she had developed a serious relationship. She had tears in her eyes when they finished their conversation, prompting her friend to ask her why she was crying. She replied that he wanted to know what she was wearing. When her friend inquired why that would make her cry, she answered, "He's the first person who's ever loved me enough to care about what I was wearing."

Her answer acknowledges an elemental principle of our social dimension. Attention is the initial response of love. Love always notices and cares about the details of the beloved's person and life. How many times have people "bored" us with the details of a loved one's person or life that excited them? What bored us excited them because they loved the individual in a way that we didn't. Attention truly is the initial response of love in human relationships.

It's also the initial response of God's love for us. We learned in Chapter 9 that God knows every possible detail about us, including the number of hairs on our heads, because He's omniscient. But His experience of them goes beyond merely knowing them to attending to them. He cares about and is engrossed in the particulars of our persons and lives. They may not matter to anyone else but they do to Him because He loves us. A mother told me with regret that her son, a freshman in college, missed the dean's list by one-tenth of a grade point. A wife related to me with delight that her husband was chosen "Employee of the Month" at his workplace. God experienced more regret and more delight than the mother and wife did. He loves us so much that nothing in our persons and lives is too small to matter to Him.

There's a third aspect of God's love. It's sacrificial action.

One of the keenest insights into the nature of love is found in a term Paul uses in 1 Thessalonians 1:3. He uses it almost "in passing" so that it's easily missed when we read the text. It's "labor of love." Commentator Leon Morris' explanation of the term is invaluable, "The word translated *kopos* denotes laborious toil, and directs our minds to unceasing hardship born for love's sake."[35] To say it another way, love desires and pursues the well-being of others over its own. It acts to meet the needs and to fulfill the desires of others and does so sacrificially to the point of hardship and even death.

Countless friends of Jesus through the ages have loved that way, but two companion texts show that it was He Himself who epitomized this radical aspect of love. In John 15:13, He states straightforwardly, "Greater love has no one than this, that one lay down his life for his friends." According to John 10:11, He practiced what He preached, "I am the good shepherd; the good shepherd lays down His life for the sheep." He voluntarily died the most painful and shameful death in human history, a substitutionary death for your sake and mine. That He did demonstrates that there is no greater love than His.

There is one, however, that's just as great. Can you think of anything more sacrificial than giving your life for others? I can. It's giving the life of one of my sons for others. If we love our children more than we do ourselves, surrendering their lives for others painfully and shamefully would be more sacrificial for us than surrendering our own. According to the most widely known verse in the Bible, John 3:16, that's exactly what Father God did, "For God so loved the world, that He gave His only begotten Son." The Father, Son, and Holy Spirit acted and acted sacrificially to the point of suffering, shame, and death for your sake and mine. There is no greater love!

This sacrificial action of God's love in combination with the other two aspects of it, emotional identification and attention, make the refrain of the old hymn "Love of God" no exaggeration:

O love of God, how rich and pure!
How measureless and strong!
It shall forevermore endure –
The saints' and angels' song.[37]

God Is Love Applied

The hymn's author is right. The love of God is the saints' song. Psychologists and sociologists tell us that humans wrestle with three issues more than any others. Who am I? Where did I come from? And where am I going? The love of God addresses the first of those, "Who am I?" That question goes to what we call our identity. Our identity refers to what defines us, to what we *objectively* and *ultimately* are.

All of us have a sense of identity or even multiple senses of identity. People at a sales conference were given the assignment to list the things that they are on a piece of paper, putting the most significant of those first. The "first" things they wrote down included failure, liar, coward, intelligent, beautiful, and fast talker to name a few. Those sales persons almost uniformly derived their identities from attributes of theirs but other sources of identity are associations, experiences, behaviors, achievements, affiliations, roles, and more. Yankee fan, conservative, patriot, pet lover, attorney, and intelligent to name a few are what various acquaintances of mine perceive themselves to be. They demonstrate that there are a variety of sources, good and bad, from which we can derive our sense of identity.

Our sense of identity strongly directs the overall tone of our lives by supporting or weakening our self-concept. Our self-concept is a principal factor in determining how we feel and act in response to people and events. A positive sense of identity fosters a healthy self-concept that makes us kind and strong. A negative sense of identify fosters an unhealthy self-concept that makes us unkind and weak or less kind and less strong. The old axiom that "Hurting people hurt people" is just one manifestation of the critical part our sense of identity plays in our day-to-day personalities and lives.

The critical part it plays impresses upon us the urgency of defining what we *objectively* and *ultimately* are. We sometimes perceive that we are what we are not. What we *objectively* are refers to what we actually are as opposed to what we mistakenly think we are or want to be. Also, we have many identities. What we *ultimately* are refers to the single most important of those. It's the single most important fact about us.

In determining what we objectively and ultimately are, some of us make the mistake of taking our identity from people. Those people may be the significant others in our lives: spouses, children, friends, co-workers, bosses, teammates, and so on. Or they may be what sociologist George Herbert Meade called "the generalized other," a mental picture of a group of unknown people out there by whom we measure ourselves. Whoever they are, some of us make what people think about us our identity. We define ourselves in terms of their opinions or perceptions about us. We're convinced that we are what we are before them, good or bad.

But we aren't. Going back to Chapter 2, God is the supreme reality of the universe, its maker, sustainer, governor, and redeemer. All other realities pale in comparison to Him, including people. His infinite superiority makes Him not anyone or anything else the true source of our identity.

Francis of Assisi knew that as well as anyone ever has and drew the valid conclusion from it. You and I are what we are before God, nothing more and nothing less.

We can take great comfort that we are in light of His love for us. What we objectively and ultimately are is the beloved of God and we should define ourselves in terms of that. We should base our identity primarily upon that reality. A spiritual director's take on the matter is dynamic and to the point: "Define yourself radically as one beloved by God. God's love for you and his choice of you constitute your worth. Accept that, and let it become the most important thing in your life."[36] It's sound advice and we need to take it. We need to perceive ourselves radically as the beloved of God and make the fact that we are and that fact alone the principal basis of our self-concept.

We need to do that and we can because of what we know. Someone in the question and answer part of a conference asked the brilliant scholar Karl Barth what the most profound doctrine of Christianity is. Everyone anxiously awaited his reply assuming it'd be some deep and esoteric theological insight, but it wasn't. He answered instead, "Jesus loves me this I know, for the Bible tells me so." Yes, God is love and I am His beloved. This I know because the Bible tells me so.

CHAPTER 13

"WHAT DO YOU SAY?"

God Is Good

As many of your parents did you, my mother taught me two prayers before any others. One was the "Now I lay me down to sleep" night time prayer. The other was the dinner table prayer that we call "saying grace," the one that most of us have said or heard said hundreds of times in our lives: "God is great; God is good; let us thank Him for our food. By His hands we all are fed. Give us Lord our daily Bread." It's a simple prayer that's often mindlessly recited and yet it's rich in truth about the nature of God. He's great, as we learned in Chapters 3-10, and He's good, as we'll learn in this one.

God Is Good Revealed

We sing a chorus that joyfully broadcasts the goodness of God with the title reflecting statement, "God is so good." You know how the lyrics go: "God is so good. God is so good. God is so good. He's so good to me." We memorialize the goodness of God with this simple sentence of God's substance because the Bible itself does. The psalmist exhorts us in Psalm 107:1 to give thanks to God for "He is good." God promises restoration to the Israelites in Jeremiah 33, prophesying in verse 11 that they would once again urge each other to say "the LORD is good." In his oracle of Nineveh in Nahum 1:7, the prophet not only lauds the power of God but revels in the fact that "the LORD is good." God is good in the same sense that He is love.

Three related Old Testament texts avow His goodness in an ecclesiastical and corporate setting. One is 1 Chronicles 16:34. King David assigned Asaph and his relatives the task of writing and publicly proclaiming a psalm of thanksgiving to fete God for bringing the Ark of the Covenant to Jerusalem. They did so urging the Israelites to "Give thanks to the Lord for He is good." David's son, Solomon built the first temple for God in Jerusalem and after the Ark of the Covenant had been placed in it, the Levitical singers broke out in song in 2 Chronicles 5:13, "He (God) indeed is good." When the Shekinah glory of God filled the temple a short time later, the Israelites prostrated themselves before Him and praised Him saying in 2 Chronicles 7:3, "Truly He is good." Notice in each text that a sense of God's goodness triggered corporate worship, indicating that it should be one of the essential elements underlying ours.

The New Testament too affirms the goodness of God. Jesus assures that a rich young man would know the implications of calling Him good by affirming in Mark 10:18, "No one is good except God alone." Perfection of goodness dwells only in Him. James notes in 1:17 of his letter that "every good thing given" comes down from "the Father of lights." God is the author of all goodness and as such must be the embodiment of goodness as well. Paul equates "what the will of God is" with "that which is good" in Romans 12:2 thereby making His will and goodness synonymous with each other. Other New Testament texts such as Romans 8:28 and 1 Timothy 4:4 recite what is good as an intended product of God's actions. The New Testament nowhere states that "God is good" but the nature and extent of its teaching on the subject make it beyond debate that He is.

God Is Good Explained

Like all of His attributes, His goodness is infinite and perfect. He's as good as it's possible to be and He will never be less "good" than He is now. Consequently, we can count on His goodness to us. We can stake our lives on it now in this life and forever in the life to come.

An analogy gets us into the core of the divine goodness. Bear in mind some of the things in day-to-day life to which we ascribe goodness. We comment how "good" a food is, how "good" the weather is, how "good" the picture on a TV screen is, and how "good" a dog is. What do we mean when we apply that word to those and countless others things? We mean that the food pleases our palate, the weather makes us comfortable, the television screen enhances our viewing experience, and the dog brings us joy without hassle. We're saying those things are good because they confer blessing or benefit upon us. God is good for the same reason.

We can think of this goodness of His in terms of what leadership expert John Maxwell calls "adding" and "subtracting" value. On the negative side, it's foreign to His nature to subtract value from creation generally and His people's lives particularly. It isn't "in Him' to take away blessings from us or to impose misfortunes upon us. His actions never leave us "worse off" than we were before. On the positive side, it's inherent in His nature to add value to creation and His people's lives. It's "in Him" to impart blessings to us and to take away misfortune from us. His actions always leave us "better off" than we were before. A simple summary of the two sides is that He always adds value to our lives and never subtracts it. He always desires and pursues what is best for creation and us.

Or does He? Some years ago, I counseled a Christian mother whose son was diagnosed with schizophrenia the day before. Overwhelmed with sadness and grief, she vowed "I'll never sing 'God Is So Good' again." Most of us can relate to her because we've been there and done that. Something bad, even catastrophic, has happened to us, leaving us to wonder about or perhaps even deny God's goodness.

In 1981, Rabbi Harold Kushner wrote a widely received book that arose from his own experience in that regard, the death of his 14 year-old son from a genetic disease. It's titled *When Bad Things Happen to Good People* and addresses the conundrum many of us have with God's goodness. If He's so good, then why do so many bad things happen to so many good or innocent people?

We must be objective and candid enough to admit that the title of Kushner's book does accurately depict the way things are. My mother was one of the finest friends Jesus ever had but I've not known or been acquainted with anyone who had a harder life than she did. It was a series of unfortunate events beyond her control. It's a fact that bad things do happen to good people, people who are disciples and friends of Jesus. It's the way things are.

But it isn't the *only* way things are. There's far more to reality than bad things happening to good people. We'd do well to take off our blinders and look at what other things are happening as well.

Let's do this first of all with reference to good people. I know a friend of Jesus who's so healthy he hasn't been to a doctor in 30 years. I know another friend of Jesus who acquired a dream job through a whole series of unlikely circumstances that had the hand of God written all over them. Those anecdotes reflect reality as accurately as Kushner's book title does. What about when *bad things don't happen to good people*? And what about when *good things happen to good people*?

Now let's peruse what things are happening to bad people. An abusive and buzzed husband had a horrible car-totaling automobile accident from which he escaped unscathed. A morally bankrupt law student was given a prized associate's position in a major city's most prestigious law firm. Those anecdotes reflect reality as accurately as Kushner's book title does. What about when *bad things don't happen to bad people*? And what about when *good things happen to bad people*.

It's imperative that we take off our blinders and look at reality broadly not narrowly. We see the following when we do: (1) Bad things happen to good people; (2) Bad things don't happen to good people; (3) Good things happen to good people; (4) Bad things don't happen to bad people; and (5) Good things happen to bad people. Those of us who look narrowly *only see* reality #1 and conclude from it that God isn't good. Those of us who look broadly *also see* realities #2, #3, #4, and #5 and conclude from them that God is good and that #1 is the consequence of sin, not any badness in Him. In assessing God's goodness, we must take all of what "happens" into account not just part of it.

What we're taking into account here is what Paul calls in 2 Corinthians 4:16-18 "the things which are seen," what happens now in our lives on earth. But to accurately assess God's goodness, we must also take into account what he calls "the things which are not seen," what will happen in our lives to come after our lives on earth. In an assuring statement that effectively rebuts arguments against God's goodness, Paul maintains that "momentary light affliction is producing for us an eternal weight of glory far beyond all comparison." No assessment of God's goodness is informed that doesn't allow for the grand and glorious eternal life that's in store for His people.

Let's get more specific. A skeptic brought up to me the absurdity of believing in a good God. He mentioned a Viet Nam veteran we both knew who had been horribly disfigured and maimed. "Can you honestly look at him," he asked me, "And say with a straight face that God is good?" Many challenge God's goodness in that way. What about the dreadful things that happen to people like being maimed, abused, tortured, expatriated, raped, and more? If God is so good, how do we explain those horrors?

I'll tell you. It's as they relate to the eternal. The eternal is the breath-taking life with breath-taking beings in a breath-taking environment and world that never ends for disciples and friends of Jesus. The meaning of events in human life is always found in what comes after them. What comes after them is that life with those beings in that environment and world.

If we're objective and sincere in our inquiry, we'll base our judgment about God's goodness on that. We see the son's schizophrenia but not only that. We also see his sick mind made whole in the eternal life to come. We see the Viet Nam veteran's disfigured body and face. We also see His body and face made perfect and whole in the eternal life to come. This isn't mere conjecture but the very promise of God Himself in Revelation 21:4: "And He will wipe away every tear from their eyes and there will no longer be any death; and there will no longer be any mourning or crying or pain; the first things have passed away." The meaning of what happens now is found in what comes later and according to this text, what comes later if we're disciples and friends of Jesus is utter and permanent goodness.

Some measure of what comes later actually comes now. We can experience something of the eternal in good times and bad by intently and persistently engaging Jesus and His kingdom at hand. The psalmist's engrossing words in Psalm 16:11 reveal what that something of the eternal is, "In Your presence is fullness of joy." Jesus echoes the psalmist's sentiment in John 15:11, charging His disciples and us that "your joy may be made full." God's presence and the fullness of joy that accompanies it together is the final good that makes heaven heaven. And He gives us a taste of it now just because He's "so good."

God Is Good Applied

The causation in that last sentence is eye-opening. God gives what is good because He is good. In the divine personality as in the human, action follows attribute. What God is directs what He does. He is good and because He is, He acts to give what is good.

James 1:17 goes straight to the heart of this reality averring without compromise that "Every good thing given and every perfect gift is from above, coming down from the Father of lights." The word "every" is all-inclusive and links the goodness of God with day-to-day life's endless "good things" and "perfect gifts" of which you and I are recipients. We know by our own ongoing experience of them what they are: the delight of a lovely sunset, the pleasure of chocolate chip cookie, the joy of a loved one's hug, the satisfaction of a job well done, the enjoyment of a warm shower, the refreshment of an ice cold drink on a hot day, the benefit of a life-changing truth, the ease of driving a car, and the comfort of an electric razor to name just a few. The "good things" and "perfect gifts" of our day-to-day experience are too numerous to keep track of them. According to James, each one comes from the beneficent hand of God. He Himself gives each one.

So "What do you say?" I once observed a grandfather in a restaurant lobby give his little grandson four quarters for the gumball and prize machines. Almost simultaneously the little boy's father asked him, "What do you say?" To which he replied, "Thank you Paw Paw." Good parents teach their children the rules of common courtesy and one of the first of those they teach is to say "Please" and "Thank you." They instruct them that it's becoming, sensible, to say "Thank you" when someone gives them something good and unbecoming, rude, not to.

This rule of common courtesy extends first and foremost to the Great Giver, God, a conclusion that logically follows from the Bible's repeated linkage of our thanksgiving with His goodness. Three texts I've already mentioned in conjunction with His goodness are clear-cut examples of this: (1) Psalm 107:1 – "Oh, give thanks to the LORD, for He is good;" (2) Jeremiah 33:11 – "Give thanks to the LORD of hosts, For the LORD is good;" and (3) 1 Chronicles 16:34 – "O give thanks to the LORD, for He is good." These texts reflect the Bible's insistence that it's appropriate to habitually thank God for His good gifts and inappropriate, even unseemly or brutish, not to.

The widespread custom of "saying grace" at meal times testifies to our grasp of this truism and our desire to live it out. But "saying grace" only at meal times is a woefully inadequate response to the goodness of God. It signals a stunted awareness of His good gifts if not an insensible attitude of ingratitude toward them. Another child's mealtime blessing launches us into larger regions of thanksgiving: "Thank you for the world so sweet. Thank you for the food we eat. Thank you for the birds that sing. Thank you God for everything." God would approve. We need to cultivate an attitude of gratitude that "says grace" for "everything," for all the person enriching and life enhancing blessings He bestows regularly upon us.

There are two strategies we can employ to cultivate an attitude of gratitude. One is to imagine what it would be like to use or experience something for the first time. Another is to imagine what our lives would be like if we permanently lost the use or experience of it. So, I remove my eyeglasses, focus on the resulting blur, and imagine how diminished my life would be if I always saw things that way. Or I put my eyeglasses back on and imagine that I'm seeing things clearly for the first time in my life and imagine how thrilled I'd be. But it isn't just eyeglasses. It's central heating, microwaves, eyesight, taste, a loved one's hug, running water, supermarkets, paved streets, a walk in the woods, washing machines, toothbrushes and toothpaste, safety razors, and showers to name just a handful of "the good things from above." We purposefully practice strategies that foster an attitude of gratitude that habitually "says grace" for the countless good things God gives us.

There's nothing difficult about how we "say grace." We express our gratitude to God through thoughts or words. I read an article titled "40 Ways to Say Thank You." They include the following: (1) "Words are powerless to express my gratitude;" (2) "Please accept my best thanks;" (3) "I thank you from the bottom of my heart;" (4) Words can't express how thankful I am;" (5) "What would I do without you;" (6) "I can't thank you enough;" and (7) "Your generosity and goodness overwhelm me."[37] We should be just as thoughtful, creative, and sincere in thanking God as we are in thanking people.

Thanking God that way is one of the central activities by which we engage Him and as such is essential to relationship with Him. Relationship with Him deepens with our thanksgivings just because of their effect upon Him and us. They delight Him and He says "You're welcome" by drawing us into the sphere of His transforming influence. Saying grace for all His blessings is an indispensable component in becoming like Him.

Because it is, it only makes good sense to heed Paul's admonition in Ephesians 5:20 for God's sake and ours, "Always giving thanks for all things in the name of our Lord Jesus Christ to God, even the Father." What do you say to God? If you're in touch with reality and wise, you'll say, "Thank you."

CHAPTER 14

"IT'S AMAZING"

God Is Gracious

One can make the case that America's favorite hymn is "Amazing Grace." It's certainly the choice of bereaved loved ones, in my experience at least. In the approximately 200 funeral services I've presided over, the song most frequently sung or played, by far, was "Amazing Grace." Its fistful of salient Biblical insights touches people, inciting confidence and hope whether things in their lives are going poorly or well.

The song's title shouts out one of those insights from the housetops, "God's grace is amazing." Dictionaries list the following words as synonyms for "amazing:" awesome, incredible, marvelous, stunning, unbelievable, and wonderful. We aren't puffing when we say that God's grace is all those things.

God Is Gracious Revealed

Statements of substance in the Bible assert God's grace just as they do His love and goodness. Exodus 22:27, 2 Chronicles 30:9, and Joel 2:13 reveal about Him that He "is gracious." His grace matches and complements His love and goodness and like them is perfect and infinite in its nature.

Statements of description buttress the Bible's statements of substance about God's grace.

In a fascinating text, Exodus 34:6, God passes in front of Moses in some sort of theophany and describes Himself as, "The LORD, the LORD God, compassionate and *gracious*, slow to anger, and abounding in lovingkindness and truth." This self-description occurs in the context of Him forgiving the Israelites for worshipping the golden calf and renewing His covenant with them. He names in this text the very foundations upon which the relationship between a perfect God and His flawed people must stand. It's His compassion, patience, love, and *graciousness*. Without those attributes of His, we would surely perish.

Centuries later, good king Hezekiah invites the scattered tribes of Israel to a peculiar Passover celebration, calling upon them in a public proclamation to "return to the LORD." If they do, he assures them in 2 Chronicles 30:9, God would reestablish them in their homeland. He then identifies the basis upon which his assurance rests, "For the LORD your God is *gracious* and compassionate, and will not turn His face away from you if you return to Him." God's graciousness is as welcome a benefit to His people as His compassion is.

And it's plentiful when they repent. Shortly after the repatriated Israelites rebuilt Jerusalem's city walls, they assembled publicly in Nehemiah 9 to rehearse God's greatness in His dealings with historical Israel. In the context of mentioning several of historical Israel's particular sins, the Levites leading the assembly proclaim in verse 17, "But You are a God of forgiveness, *gracious* and compassionate, slow to anger and abounding in lovingkindness; and you did not forsake them." Derek Kidner's succinct commentary on this statement encapsulates their message, "Sin abounds, grace superabounds."[38] It's reminiscent of Paul's storied dictum in Romans 5:20 that "where sin increased, grace abounded all the more." The power and reach of sin is measured. The power and reach of grace is measureless.

God's grace is mentioned in these and a host of other texts approximately 170 times, making it one of the Bible's motto-themes. It occupies a place of prominence in both the Bible and Christian hymnology rivaling that of its cousins, love and goodness. Those who comprehend and thereby treasure what it is would expect no less.

God Is Gracious Explained

Comprehending it begins with a fundamental truth. The warp and woof of grace is action. It's God acting to give or to do *something good* that *we don't deserve* or not to give or to do *something bad* that *we do deserve*. Were there no action of God there would be no grace with the result that human life generally and your life and mine individually would collapse under the weight of our world's fallenness and people's sin. So-called "wellness" is a popular theme in our cultural context but most people, Christians and non-Christians alike, are oblivious to a simple fact of life. Unwellness (monotony, poverty of soul, and pain) would be the totality of our life experience if God wasn't giving His grace and we weren't receiving it in regular doses. Any kind and level of wellness we experience is achieved by consuming it in one or another of its three facets.

The first facet is common grace. It's common in that God acts on behalf of those who reject Jesus just as He does those who receive Him. Reformed theologian Louis Berkhof construes common grace as God's action that "curbs the destructive power of sin, maintains in a measure the moral order of the universe, thus making an orderly life possible, distributes in varying degrees gifts and talents among men, promotes the development of science and art, and showers untold blessings upon the children of men."[39] As Berkhof's depiction indicates, three basic actions comprise God's common grace.

One is that He acts to restrain the effects of the ever occurring sins people commit and the mistakes they make.

Calculate the sum total of people's wicked, selfish, thoughtless, foolish, uninformed, misinformed, and negligent acts in the course of a common day. I marvel when I do that one can reliably buy a television set that actually works, eat without getting food poisoning, drive without incident, sit in stands that don't collapse, have successful surgeries, live without being physically assaulted, and much more. It's truly remarkable that our world works as well as it does. The logical explanation is God's common grace – His action to curb the detrimental consequences of the sins and mistakes that permeate ordinary human life. Human life and our individual lives would be dystopian without it.

A second action of God's common grace is material and physical provision for all. In Proverbs 29:13, the wise man boasts that "The poor man and the oppressor have this in common: the LORD gives light to the eyes of both." The Bible decries oppressors of the poor as recipients of God's wrath and yet He gives them light, by way of the sun, just as He does the poor they oppress. Jesus picks up on this thought and reiterates it in Matthew 5:45, "for He (God) causes His sun to rise on the evil and the good, and sends rain on the righteous and unrighteous." The wicked are no less "well off" materially and physically than the righteous. We might bemoan what we perceive to be the injustice of the health and wealth of the evildoers of the world but in reality we shouldn't. They're living breathing testimonies of God's common grace.

God's common grace is comprised of a third action. Usually called "prevenient grace," it's the Holy Spirit working in people's minds and hearts to enlighten and convict them. The result is that they, at some point in their fallen state, have the ability to decide for God instead of against Him. I'm calling this "common" grace because, unlike pure Calvinists, I believe the Holy Spirit enlightens and convicts all people not just the "elect" as they define them. God doesn't wish "for any to perish" (2 Peter 3:9). On the contrary, He "desires all men to be saved and to come to the knowledge of the truth" (1 Timothy 2:4). Consequently, He works enough in the mental, emotional, volitional, and bodily processes of all so they can be if they choose.

The Second Coming of Jesus concludes common grace as I've just explained it. When He comes again, God will "deal out retribution to those who do not know God and to those who do not obey the gospel of our Lord Jesus" (2 Thessalonians 1:8). It's pay day for rejecters of Jesus to whom God will justly give the "bad" they do deserve in place of the "good" they don't.

There's a second facet of God's grace. One is common grace. A second is saving grace. You're probably familiar with the term "saving faith," one that we regularly employ to communicate how we're saved. We must be careful though lest it mislead the people to whom we speak it. They might infer from it that our faith in Jesus saves us when in reality it doesn't. It's necessary but not enough. In the end, our faith doesn't save us. God's grace does. It's saving grace.

Paul's famed salvation formula in Ephesians 2:8-10 pinpoints with precision the parts our faith and God's grace play in salvation. We're saved "*by* grace" (verse 8), "*through* faith" (verse 8), and "*for* good works" (verse 10). Paul placing grace first before faith and attaching the prepositions he did to them, both of which I believe were intentional, indicates that God's grace is the medium that makes our faith effectual. If He weren't gracious, our faith, however how rich and deep, wouldn't save us. But He is and so it does.

The dynamics of saving grace are found in the finished work of Jesus and what it accomplished in the realm of God's kingdom. What it accomplished is what is called "unlimited atonement." Simply put, Jesus was born of a virgin, lived a sinless life, died a substitutionary death, and rose from the dead *for the sins of everyone* who ever lives.

As a result of this finished work of His, God has three options available to Him. #1 – He can justly damn everyone because all have sinned and they deserve it. #2 – He can justly save everyone even though all have sinned and they don't deserve it. And #3 – He can justly elect to save those who decide to receive Jesus and to damn those who decide to reject Him.

Those are God's three options and according to the Bible, He chose the third. He elects to give to those of us who decide in faith to follow Jesus the good we don't deserve, salvation, and not to give us the bad we do deserve, damnation. Since giving what is good to those who don't deserve it and not giving what is bad to those who do deserve it is the very essence of grace, there's no doubting it. We're saved "by grace" (Romans 3:24; Titus 3:7).

God's grace doesn't end when we're saved but continues and increases. There is a third facet of it that becomes operative in our ongoing lives with God. It's enabling grace.

Even a cursory reading of the teachings of Jesus and the New Testament authors impresses it upon us that God expects us to be and do much of what is beyond us. Having studied the kingdom life that Jesus pictures in His Sermon on the Mount (Matthew 5-7), a Christian approached me, threw up his hands in despair, and cried out, "No one can live like that." He was wrong! I do concede that no one, including you and me, can live like that in his or her own power. We cannot in our own competence and strength be the kind of person and live the kind of life that participation in God's kingdom requires of us.

But we can be that kind of person and live that kind of life by the grace of God. It's an issue about which the Bible doesn't leave us guessing. His gracious actions in us and upon us enable us to give liberally (2 Corinthians 9:8), stand strong in the troubles and trials of life (2 Corinthians 12:9), minister effectively (Romans 1:5; 1 Corinthians 15:10; 2 Timothy 2:1), perform miracles (Acts 6:8), grow in character (Hebrews 13:9), find help in need (Hebrews 4:16), and overcome sin and Satan (James 4:6). We know from texts like these and others and our own personal experiences with God that His grace is the primary active force in our spiritual, psychological, physical, and social realities if we're disciples of Jesus.

Philippians 1:6-7 is a fine summary statement of what God's enabling grace ultimately accomplishes for us. In verse 6, Paul attests his confidence that God "who began a good work in you will perfect it until the day of Christ Jesus." "Good work" refers to God acting in us and upon us to make our character and lives "kingdom-like." "Will perfect it" refers to Him doing so continually all of our days on earth. We become increasingly "kingdom-like" as a result until finally, at the Second Coming of Jesus, the Holy Spirit makes us perfectly that in our resurrection bodies. Paul proceeds in verse 7 to couch this perfecting work of God in us as you and I being "partakers of grace" or more specifically, "partakers of enabling grace." The word "partakers" means "to take a share" of something, which is in this verse God's grace. The logical conclusion to which it leads both surprises and humbles us. Those of us in relationship with God take a far bigger share of His grace than those out of it do. We're ravenous consumers of it. We're the fortunate beneficiaries of His unremitting actions on our behalf to transform us, to forgive us, to empower us, and to enhance our efforts.

When all the dust of learning about grace has settled, we realize that its actions are more far-reaching than many of us realize. They extend beyond forgiving the repentant (saving faith) to physically sustaining everyone (common grace) and perfecting disciples and friends of Jesus (enabling grace). In view of those actions, it's no stretch of the truth to call grace "amazing."

God Is Gracious Applied

There's something else I'd call it, "greater." If I were developing a watchword for it in fact, it'd be "Grace is greater!" It's greater than the most formidable foe of humans. Julia Johnston wrote a favorite hymn over a century ago the title of which celebrates to what I'm referring, "Grace Greater than Our Sin."

No doctrine of the Christian gospel is more widely written and spoken about than the doctrine of sin. The Bible does draw a critical distinction between "sin" and "sins" and as always is right in doing so. A well-worn aphorism picks up on the distinction and frames it in a way that clarifies the relationship between the two. We aren't sinners because we sin; we sin because we're sinners. It's a distinction we need to pursue if we're to understand the greatness of God's grace.

Sins, also called transgressions and iniquities in the Bible, are attitudes and actions that are contrary to God's nature and His Biblical commandments that reflect it. Acting impatiently in traffic is a sin because it's contrary to an attribute of His, His patience. Or committing adultery is a sin because it's contrary to an attribute of His, His triunity. Sins occur when people think and act in ways that violate the nature and commandments of God.

The people I'm talking about here are all of us. John gets straight to the point in 1 John 1:10, "If we say that we have not sinned, we make Him (God) a liar and His word is not in us." We make Him a liar because He tells us in His written word the Bible that we have. Isaiah 53:5, for instance, insists that "*All* of us like sheep have gone astray, *each* of us has turned to his own way." Paul concurs in his oft-repeated pronouncement in Romans 3:23 that "*all* have sinned and fall short of the glory of God." The Bible in these verses and others "makes no bones" about it. Sins aren't peculiar to select individuals but are universal to everyone. Jesus is the only person who ever was sinless and who ever will be. It's a sobering thought that the history of our own personal lives is dotted with sin after sin, in the thousands if we'd calculate the number of them.

Taking the sheer number of our sins into account, it's seems ironic that many if not most of us, and I'm addressing Christians here, don't lose any sleep over them. We gossip, get angry, grumble, or seek praise and don't feel guilty that we did. If the truth be told, many of us take those common sins and others like them lightly.

A dichotomy we draw in our minds is usually the culprit behind this cavalier attitude of ours.

Thoughtfully answer two questions. First, how many professing Christians would physically assault someone for criticizing them? The answer is "almost none." Second, how many professing Christians would verbally assault someone for criticizing them? The answer is, and I'm not being unduly pessimistic here, "almost all." Based on conversations I've had with scores of professing Christians, I believe the difference in response lies in what they perceive to be the harm that's done. It's great enough in the first scenario (physical assault) that they refrain from inflicting it but slight enough in the second (verbal assault) that they don't.

The lesson is that we tend to take common sins lightly because we think they're inconsequential. That's the idea behind the term we use, "a little white lie," and I draw your attention to the word "little." We tend to distinguish between little sins and big ones, determined by the harm that's done. A church member, a traveling salesman, confessed his plight to me: "I'm not worried about lusting. I have enough trouble when I'm on the road not committing adultery." His candid confession is representative of what many of us think about sins. They're little when the harm is slight and so, we don't take them seriously. It's the idea, "No harm; no foul." In contrast, they're big when the harm is great with the result that we do take them seriously.

The Bible, however, begs to differ, emphasizing in texts like James 2:10-11 that there are no little sins. It maintains that all sins without exception are big ones because each has the same singular catastrophic consequence that's part and parcel of the finished work of Jesus.

Bill O'Reilly published a series of bestselling books about the murder of historical personalities: Abraham Lincoln, John F. Kennedy, George Patton, and Jesus. He was right to include Jesus in his "Killing" franchise because He was in fact killed in cold blood. He was murdered in the same sense that Abraham Lincoln and John F. Kennedy were.

The initial and compelling question when someone is murdered is "Who did it?" The popularity of whodunit books resides in the consuming curiosity that grips people when it isn't easily answered. But no whodunit book could be written about the death of Jesus because we know with certainty who did it. You and I did! You and I killed Him as surely as the Roman centurion who nailed Him to the cross did. Harboring no illusions about this damning truth about us, Martin Luther commented that each of us carries the nails of the cross in our pockets.

The unique nature of Jesus' death on the cross takes away any mystery about who perpetrated it. Biblical language employed in texts such as Isaiah 53:5 and 1 Peter 2:14 portray it as a kind of death that no other person has died or ever will die. It was more than a martyr's death as evidenced by Jesus' struggle in Gethsemane (Luke 22:41-44). It was a substitutionary death. He took all of our sins into Himself and paid the penalty for them that we should have paid so that we wouldn't have to.

We need to come to grips with the horrifying implication of this. Your sins and mine put Jesus on the cross and I mean that metaphysically not metaphorically. The old hymn asks, "Were you there when they crucified my Lord." Yes, we were in that each of our sins put Him there. A long time Christian gossiped about her pastor to several others and me. If no other human ever sinned and she sinned only that once, Jesus would still have died on the cross for that sin of hers. The same is true of each individual sin of ours no matter how little it seems, whether it's a lustful look or a little white lie. That reality puts all our sins in their larger unseen context, which is the cross. And in that context, there are no little sins. Each and every one is a big one instead because it caused the ultimate harm – the death of God's perfect and innocent Son, Jesus. In the truest sense of the word, you and I killed Him.

It would seal our fate that we did if it weren't for God's saving grace. Hebrews 12:24 elaborates on the subject with a razor sharp insight about the blood of Jesus that was shed on the cross. His blood "speaks better than the blood of Abel."

Genesis 4:10 records some of the most chilling words in the Bible. God confronts Cain, who had murdered his brother Abel, with the words, "The voice of your brother's blood is crying to Me from the ground." God employs a figure of speech here that we ourselves also use in the context of perpetuated wrongs, personification. After the 9/11 attacks on the Twin Towers, a newscaster said, "The attack on the Twin Towers is a wrong that cries out to be righted." It's the same idea in Genesis 4:10. This verse pictures Abel's blood crying out to God from the ground, raising the provocative question, "What did it say?" Hebrew tradition tells us. It said "vengeance," which is, I believe, the correct interpretation of the verse. The blood of Abel did in fact cry out for vengeance. It called on God to right the wrong of his murder by giving Cain exactly what he deserved for doing it, death.

That interpretation gives us the reference point we need for understanding Hebrews 12:24. It employs the same figure of speech God did in Genesis 4:10. It personifies the blood of Jesus by stating that it "speaks." Like Abel's, it cries out to Father God, again raising the provocative question, "What did it say?" The word "better" in verse 24 implies the answer. The blood of Jesus speaks better than – the opposite of – the blood of Abel thereby signifying what it says, "grace." *The blood of Abel cried out for vengeance. The blood of Jesus cries out for grace.* It calls on Father God not to give us what we deserve for committing sins that murdered Him, spiritual and eternal death, but to forgive those sins and give us what we don't deserve, spiritual and eternal life.

And that's what He does. He forgives our sins when we repent so that it's as if we never even committed them. The Bible formulates this reality as Jesus' blood making "atonement" (Leviticus 17:11; Hebrews 9:12-14). The word "atonement" connotes that His blood either obliterates or covers our sins with the result that God regards and treats us as if we hadn't committed them.

We can liken the outcome of God's grace with the outcome of a legal procedure called expungement. When a person pleads to a crime or is convicted of one, the state records his name and crime in its database. But for a certain category of crimes and under certain conditions, he can eventually file a motion for expungement with the court. If it's granted, the state removes his name and crime from its database so that there's no public record of it. As far as the state's concerned, it's as if he never committed it. You quickly see the application to God and our sins. When we repent, He expunges them as definitively as the state does and regards and treats us as if we never committed them.

The absoluteness of His forgiveness, as the expungement analogy shows, leaves us in good standing with Him and illuminates the power and reach of His grace. It's greater than all our sins.

It's also greater than our sin. Sin is the fallen self-centered nature with which we're born and includes all the impulses, urges, and inclinations to evil that dwell in our minds, hearts, and bodies. At one juncture in my life, I envied peers who eclipsed me and secretly wished they hadn't. Envy is only one of the many inclinations to evil that reside in us and is a product of our fallen nature. I've experienced the directing force of the sin that indwells us and so have you.

The self-centered nature that is sin is a permanent occupant in the interior of our being and cannot be evicted. It's an unruly tenant that must be subdued if we're to be the kingdom people living the kingdom lives that God desires of us. It must be subdued and according to Paul in Romans 6:12-14, it can be.

He exhorts us in the opening line of verse 12, "Do not let sin reign in your mortal body." That he does assumes that we can do otherwise, which is the truth. The majority of people it seems let sin reign in their bodies and lives or to say it differently, they learn to live with it. After a battery of tests, a specialist prognosticated that the ringing in the ears of his patient wouldn't go away. "There's nothing we can do about it," he said, "You'll just have to learn to live with it." Most people take that same approach when it comes to sin. They learn to live with it.

A popular bit of bumper sticker theology is a constant reminder to us that they do, "Christians aren't perfect, just forgiven." This widely used slogan reminds me of a highly respected pastor-televangelist who illustrated the difference between Christians and non-Christians this way. Non-Christians, he said, get angry and lash out at others but not feeling guilty they did, don't repent. Christians on the other hand get angry and lash out at others but feeling guilty they did, repent and are forgiven.

The commonality of the slogan and the televangelist's illustration is in approaching sin as something Christians have to live with. As the word "just" in the slogan implies, their sin (their fallen nature) fates them to commit sins with the same frequency and in the same ways that non-Christians do. But unlike non-Christians, they repent and are forgiven. They have no more control over their sin than non-Christians do. But they do have control over the effects of the sins to which it leads by immediately seeking and getting forgiveness.

That's their strategy for dealing with sin and it doesn't take a rocket scientist to figure out to what it leads. They "sin in word, thought, or deed every day" as the conscience soothing maxim to which people recurrently turn contends. They lie, covet, divorce, lust, get angry, gossip and so on as non-Christians do. They allow sin to reign and learn to live with it.

But they don't have to because God's grace is greater than our sin – greater than the fallen self-centered nature that dwells in us. His gracious action in us enables us to win over sin. You don't have to take my word for it. You can take Paul's in Romans 6.

In verses 3-7, he teaches in some detail what God's gracious action in us is about. When we apprentice ourselves to Jesus, we're united with Him in the likeness of His death and resurrection. It's another way of saying that we enter into an experiential union with Him. In that union, He infuses the same power of the Holy Spirit that raised Him from the dead into us and sustains it there. At that point, we have two powers in us, each of which we're capable of turning to moment by moment: a sin power and a greater power of the Holy Spirit.

With this new divine power now available to us, we don't have to just live with sin. By consistently turning to it, we're able to win over sin. We aren't limited to controlling the effects of the sins to which it leads. As impudent as it may sound, we're set free to conquer it. The insistence and intensity of Paul's language in Romans 6 itself removes any doubt that we are: (1) Verse 2 – "died to sin"; (2) Verse 6 – "our body of sin might be done away with"; (3) Verse 6 – "no longer slaves to sin"; (4) Verse 7 – "freed from sin"; (5) Verse 12 – "do not let sin reign"; and (6) Verse 14 – "sin shall not be master over you." If Paul didn't mean it, he wouldn't have said it. We can win over sin.

That doesn't mean we'll ever be perfect, sinless, because we won't be in our lives on earth. But let's face it. There's a lot of wiggle room between "just forgiven" on the one hand and "perfect" on the other. As we live from the power of God's gracious action in us, we increasingly move further from "just forgiven" and closer to "perfect" until sinning is the exception and acting rightly the rule in our persons and lives.

I refer you to my earlier confession that at one point in my life I envied peers who eclipsed me and wished they hadn't. That's no longer true of me. I've grown in grace as we say it so that I now root for my peers to eclipse me and rejoice when they do. I'm not perfect by any stretch of the imagination but I'm not just forgiven either. As I consistently turn to God's action and power in me, sin is decreasing and righteousness increasing in my person and life.

Paul's exhortation in Romans 6:12 sets the bar for you and me. We must not let sin reign over us. It isn't an overpowering force that we're pretty much helpless against. It's a force that we can overcome in and through the power of God's enabling grace.

We overcome it not solely but primarily by carrying out Paul's command in Romans 6:12. On the negative side, we don't present our body parts as instruments of unrighteousness or sin. We don't use them to achieve what is evil. On the positive side, we do present them as instruments of righteousness. We do use them to achieve what is good.

Operating in the confines of Paul's command is the assumption that doing what is good and not doing what is bad isn't as hard in most of the circumstances of real life as we make it out to be. In a prayer meeting I attended with a group of pastors, one pleaded: "Oh Lord, doing what the world wants is so easy but doing what you want is so hard. Help us." I disagree. Doing not all but most of what God wants, the good and not the evil, isn't "so hard." Most of our temptations are simple scuffles with sin that don't take what one blogger calls "super heroic willpower" to overcome. With God's grace in us enabling us, all it takes is the intent to obey Him. First, we learn what He says. Second, we recognize when occasions arise to do what He says. And third, we assert our grace empowered selves and do it. The cosmic force of sin is for the most part no match for disciples of Jesus who intend to do what is good and right. Disciples who are growing in grace eventually prevail.

It's a sensational claim I know but it's categorically true. Grace is greater than our sin and the sins to which it leads – and all the other challenges we face in our fallen world. One of the stanza's of America's favorite hymn summarizes well its overcoming power: "Through many dangers, toils, and snares, I have already come. 'Tis grace that brought us safe thus far and grace will lead me home." We aren't exaggerating when we say about God's grace, "It's amazing."

CHAPTER 15

"100% PURE"

God Is Holy

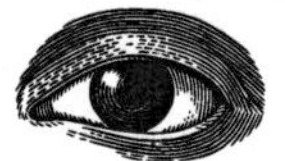

One of the most identifiable advertising slogans in history is Ivory Soap's "It's 99 and 44/100 pure." Did you ever wonder of what the other 56/100% consists? Apparently it's 11/100% alkali, 28/100% carbonates, and 17/100% mineral matter, if you care. You probably don't care but my point is that Ivory Soap's maker and customers consider it important that it's almost pure.

99 and 44/100% pure may describe Ivory Soap but it doesn't describe God because He's 100% pure. Ivory Soap is almost pure chemically. God is wholly pure morally. He's holy in other words!

God Is Holy Revealed

Preachers and Christian leaders in the feel good environment of our day relegate the reality of God's holiness to a bygone era and flat out ignore it. The Bible doesn't. It highlights it as an attribute of His character in both the Old and New Testaments.

Celebrating God delivering them from the Egyptian chariots at the Red Sea, Moses and the Israelites sing in Exodus 15:11, "Who is like You among the gods, O LORD? Who is like You, majestic in holiness?" Both questions are rhetorical, the implied answer being "No one is like You." Their song in verses 1-21 paints God as the incomparable One who is unlike anyone or anything else that exists. One of the ways that He's incomparable is in His holiness, which elevates Him above all the blemishes and flaws that characterize the entirety of creation. His holiness was the basis of Him judging Egypt and redeeming Israel.

Soon after their exodus from Egypt, the Israelites spent a year at Mount Sinai where God gave them the law recorded in Exodus and Leviticus. In Leviticus 19:2, He underscores the foundation upon which all His commandments in that law rest and the aim He expects them to pursue in response to it, "You shall be holy, for I the LORD your God am holy." God's holiness is at the root of His commandments and our obedience to those commandments is the outworking of our holiness in return.

The psalmist gifts us with what may be the strongest statement on God's holiness in the entire Bible. He dedicates the whole of his psalm, Psalm 99, to the praise of the divine holiness and its effects on us. A refrain of God's substance in verses 3, 5, and 9 ties its contents together, "Holy is He." Those contents accentuate the distance between God and humans morally and ontologically and are a spur to us to praise Him with joy on the one hand and to fear Him with awe on the other. They impress upon us that while we shouldn't despair of God's grace, we shouldn't trade on it or take it for granted either. He is holy and will judge and punish our unholiness because He is.

Angels are as awed by God's holiness as the psalmist was. Isaiah 6:3 records that one Seraphim calls out to another, "Holy, Holy, Holy, is the LORD of hosts." The triple repetition of a word is the strongest superlative in the Hebrew language. The angels are saying that God is utterly holy! Isaiah is in concord with the angels. His favorite designation of God in his book, one that he uses 26 times, is "the Holy

One of Israel," showing the lofty place he gives divine holiness in his mind and ministry.

While few would consider Mary the mother of Jesus in Isaiah's league as a person in the know, her Magnifcat in Luke 1:46-55 shows she was no theological slouch. She firmly grasps the perfections of God's nature, specifically His power (verse 49,) holiness (verse 49), and grace (verse 50). She also possesses insight into how those perfections work in union to direct His dealings with nations and individuals, including her (verses 51-55). For our purposes, notice her linkage of holiness with mercy or grace in verses 49-50, teaching that they complement not oppose each other. God is gracious in His holiness and holy in His graciousness.

Revelation 4:8, resembling the Isaiah 6:3 text, once again takes us beyond the human understanding of God's holiness to the angelic. The four living creatures of verses 6-7, who probably symbolize the highest of all created beings, ceaselessly cry out, "HOLY, HOLY, HOLY is the LORD GOD, THE ALMIGHTY, WHO WAS AND WHO IS AND WHO IS TO COME." Their repetition of the word "HOLY" in the context of verses 1-5 denotes the matchless excellence of nature that is peculiar to Him. It's that holiness or excellence of nature that enables Him to be the arbiter of the destinies of the church and the world as presented in the subsequent chapters of Revelation.

It's readily apparent from the texts I've explained and many others that the Bible doesn't prevaricate about God's holiness. His holiness looms large on its pages from beginning to end. It's a Biblical emphasis that entreats us to explore the depths of its nature and actions.

God Is Holy Explained

The Hebrew word translated "holy" means "to be separated or cut off from" and the Greek word means "different'" or "set apart." That God is holy means that He is separated or set apart from something, actually, two things.

The first is creation itself. We use another word to communicate this aspect of His holiness. It's "transcendent." The nature of His being transcends the nature of everything else that exists in that, as I explained in Chapter 1, He's the only one of His kind.

But it isn't transcendence with which most of us associate God's holiness. It's moral purity instead. When we say He's holy, we normally mean He's morally pure. So, to understand His holiness we need to understand purity.

A federal agency, the Food and Drug Administration (FDA), assists us in doing so by way of analogy. One of the functions of the FDA is to assure the purity of foods that Americans consume. It carries out that function by establishing detailed guidelines for how adulterated particular foods are allowed to be. Since foods in America are mass harvested, processed, and packaged, there will always be what the FDA calls "defects" or "foreign matter" in what is sold on grocery store shelves such as insects, insect parts, rodent hairs, larvae (maggots), rodent feces, mammal feces, bone material, mold, rust, and cigarette butts. The FDA serves to protect customers by confining the extent of those defects to what is safe for consumption.

An example is worth a thousand words in exposing what we're up against here but I warn you, don't read the example that follows if you're squeamish. It's the specific FDA guideline for peanut butter:

Defect	Action Level
Insect filth	Average of 30 or more insect fragments per 100 grams
Rodent filth	Average of 1 or more rodent hairs per 100 grams
Grit	Gritty taste and water insoluble organic residue is more than 25 mg per 100 grams

The FDA drafts guidelines like this one for a wide variety of foods all the way alphabetically from "Allspice, Ground" to "Wheat Flour."

To wrap our minds around the FDA's detailed regulation of foods is to wrap our minds around what purity is. To be pure means to be "uncontaminated." It's foods without insects, rodent hairs, and maggots; baseball infields without stones; gardens without weeds; air without fumes; soap without alkali, carbonates, and mineral matter; and pharmaceutical drugs without "particulates" such as glass, rubber, aluminum, plastic, and wood. Things are pure when they're without contaminants.

We can quickly see from that definition of the word "pure" how it came to be applied and appropriately so to morality. Human character and behavior can be corrupted by the synonymous words that the Bible calls "sin" or "evil" just as matter can be corrupted by contaminants. To be morally pure, therefore, means for character and behavior to be "separated from" or "without" sin or evil.

It's in this sense that God is holy. That He is holy means that He is morally pure. This moral purity of His has two aspects.

One is that He's utterly separated from evil. There isn't even the slightest degree of any moral wrong of any kind in Him. Let's think of human holiness for a moment. Imagine you or I murdering a baby in cold blood. We can't imagine that because we are, in our natures, 99.44% separated from murder. It isn't in us to murder a baby. With that in mind, contemplate the tiniest evil you can think of like telling a little white lie to spare someone's feelings. God is less inclined to do that than we are inclined to murder a baby. He is in fact not inclined at all to do that. As Titus 1:2 says it, He "cannot lie." We can substitute any particular evil, no matter how minimal its effects, for the word "lie" in that verse. He cannot do any evil no matter how slight. He never thinks, feels, or does what is morally wrong because He can't. He is in His nature 100% separated from any evil of any kind. Or to say it another way, He's 0% morally bad and wrong.

God's purity has a second aspect. He's 100% morally good and right. Let return to human holiness. Imagine you or I being honest and paying for a Milky Way instead of shoplifting it. We can imagine that because we are in our natures 99.44% honest. It's in us to pay for a Milky Way. Now bring to mind the highest good you can think of – like giving your life to preserve or promote the life of another. God is more inclined to do that than we are to pay for the Milky Way. He is in fact fully inclined to do that and in the person of Jesus did. He always thinks, feels, and does what is morally good and right because He cannot do otherwise. He is in His nature 100% morally pure.

I'd quickly interject here that the analogies I just used are imperfect, even inadequate ones. It's fundamentally true that God's holiness isn't just human holiness advanced. It's so different in nature than human holiness that we know nothing that's even remotely like it. But once again, we attempt to understand the best we can and the analogies are helpful aids in doing so. We glean from them what it means that God is holy. He isn't, like Ivory Soap, 99.44% pure. He's all good and no evil, all right and no wrong. He's 100%
morally pure.

God Is Holy Applied

Discerning how God's holiness applies to us is the simplest of matters because the Bible comes right out and tells us. It states unequivocally, "You shall be holy, for I the LORD your God am holy" (Leviticus 19:2; 11:44; 1 Peter 1:16). These texts require little thought to interpret. God is holy and we should be too.

When God commands us, He equips us and this decree is no exception. We can in the real world of our day-to-day lives be holy people. Peter teaches us how we can be in the verses immediately preceding the 1 Peter 1:16 text.

He writes in verse 13 about "the grace to be brought to you at the revelation of Jesus Christ." The word "grace" refers to God's enabling grace that was discussed in Chapter 13. The prepositional phrase "at the revelation of Jesus" refers to His first coming to earth. And the word "brought" is actually a present participle that should be translated "is being brought." Pulling all of this together, Peter instructs us here that God's enabling grace, activated by the birth, life, death, and resurrection of Jesus, began working in us when we decided to follow Him. Its work in us is our "hope" of "being holy" in "all behavior," verse 15, leaving no room for doubt that the development of holiness in us is primarily the work of God.

But we must do our part by participating in that work of His. Peter gives definition to what our part is also in verse 13. He exhorts us to "prepare your minds for action, keep sober in spirit." The KJV translates the word "prepare" literally and correctly to mean "gird up the loins." It's a metaphor. First century men in the Middle East wore long gowns that they pulled up whenever energetic effort required it. Our modern equivalent is "roll up your sleeves" and that's the idea behind the clause "gird up the loins." It's to pull up our gown, to roll up our sleeves, and get to work. It's to "mean business" in other words. That's the gist of the metaphor and what we have to do to be holy. We have to mean business – in two respects.

The first respect is in our "minds." Peter reinforces his admonition to "prepare your minds" in verse 13 with the admonition to "keep sober" that immediately follows it. The word "sober" connotes alertness or mindfulness thereby clarifying what Peter intends to say. We must be always mindful of what is holy and unholy.

Being mindful is probably a greater challenge than most of us think it is because of our tendency to normalize sins. Psychologically, we have the capacity to adjust downward so that the over time the most abnormal realities, including sins, seem normal to us. Those sins are committed so often by so many people that we begin to view them as standard fare in human life.

I personally knew the pastor of a Bible-believing megachurch who was as prideful, angry, and malicious as he was successful. He was incessantly at odds with people and routinely imposed his will on them to get his own way. His behavior became so intolerable that his church's governing board finally forced him to resign. It then wrote a congregational letter explaining why it did and stressed in it that it wasn't because of a "moral failure" on his part, to quote their letter. Reading between the lines, the board equated the term "moral failure" with "sexual sin" not pride, anger, and malice and knew the congregation would too.

The board's choice of terminology and the congregation's interpretation of it demonstrate a catastrophic change that has occurred in the minds of even Bible-believing Christians. In their view, sins like pride, anger, malice, gossip, deceit, greed, gluttony and resentment to name a few aren't moral failures. They're things all of us naturally do and because they are, must be expected and even tolerated.

But they are moral failures just as drunkenness, adultery, homosexuality, theft, and murder are in nature if not effect. And the first thing we must do to be holy is to perceive them that way. We must always be alert to and mindful of what's holy and unholy in the world and in us. What God in the Bible views as moral, we must view as moral. What God in the Bible views as immoral, we must view as immoral. We must do so even if the culture or even the church around us doesn't. Being holy requires that we mean business in our minds.

It also requires that we mean business in what Peter calls our "behavior" in verse 15. He doesn't leave us clueless here but gives us the direction we need about how to do that in verse 14. On the positive side, to mean business in our behavior means we purposefully are "obedient" to God. On the negative side, it means we purposefully "do not conform to former lusts." The operative word "purposefully" shows that meaning business in our behavior is a matter of intention. Intention goes straight to the holiness or unholiness that drives our day-to-day lives.

William Law recognized this in his classic book *A Serious Call to a Devout and Holy Life* by devoting Chapters II and III to the importance and effects of intention. His words might offend the sensibilities of the more thin-skinned among us but they deserve and urgently need to be heard. Referring to the intention to please God in all our actions, he wrote as follows: "It was this general intention that made the primitive Christians such eminent examples of devotion . . . And if you will stop here and ask yourself why you are not so devoted as the primitive Christians, your own heart will tell you that it is neither through ignorance or inability but purely because you never thoroughly intended it."[40]

Law didn't underestimate or undervalue the power of intention in the context of God's enabling grace and neither should we. Why do Christians gossip? They don't intend not to. Why do they rejoice when others do better than they do? They intend to. Why don't they give good for evil? They don't intend to. Why do they wait patiently? They intend to. Intention is considerably more powerful and far-reaching than many of us give it credit. To be holy, we must intend holy behavior.

There's nothing abstract or vague about how we intend it. First, we study the Bible and learn what it says specifically is morally right and wrong. Second, we try and train our best to do the right and not to do the wrong in the circumstance before us. Doing so is called "purposeful obedience" but whatever we call it, the intention that is essential to holiness underlies it.

We see then that there's nothing esoteric about 1 Peter 1:13-16. Its simple message is that God calls us to be holy and we can be. The means by which we can be are the power of God's enabling grace supported by our commitment to mean business in our minds and in our behavior. Carrying out those means, we can reach a high level of holiness or moral purity that those apart from Jesus can't even approach. But we in our fallen state can never be as pure as God is because He's "Holy! Holy! Holy!" He's 100% morally pure.

CHAPTER 16

"THE BEGINNING OF INTELLIGENCE"

God Is Wrathful

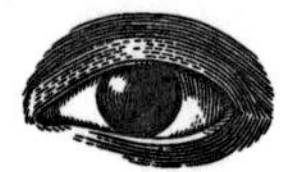

Few Christians have any aversion at all to any aspects of God's character, save one. That one is that He's wrathful. In my view, wrath isn't an attribute of His but an expression of an attribute of His, His holiness, and I'll treat it as that in this chapter. But whether it's an attribute or an expression of an attribute, it's obvious to the observant among us that Christians in general are uncomfortable in addressing God's wrath. They seem ashamed that it's part of Christian doctrine and belief, regarding it as a blotch that reflects poorly on His character. I've personally noticed that Christian preaching, teaching, writing, and conversing revel in His love, for instance, but largely downplay or outright ignore His wrath. It's the forbidden subject in our Christian communities today.

God Is Wrathful Revealed

In the Bible though, it's a principal emphasis. The Old and New Testaments refer to it in one way or another over 600 times, making it as thoroughly attested if not more so than any other Biblical truth, including God's love. Acclaimed theologian A.W. Pink rightly affirmed that "A study of the concordance will show that there are more references in

Scripture to the anger, fury, and wrath of God, than there are to His love and tenderness."[41] The sheer number of texts that speak of God's wrath to us makes it a dominant Biblical theme that we must search out and understand.

In 1:2 of the book named after Him, the prophet Nahum warns the wicked people of Nineveh what about God will be their undoing, "The LORD is avenging and wrathful." He is as wrathful as He is loving, good, and gracious and will act accordingly to avenge, that is, to deliver the oppressed and punish the oppressor.

God's words to Job's three friends in Job 42:7 contain a core truth about His wrath that underlay His dealings with Nineveh, "My wrath is kindled against you." It isn't an arbitrary expression of His holiness that comes out of nowhere. It's "kindled" instead, a voluntary reaction of His to the wickedness of humans.

A penitential psalm, Psalm 38:1, pulls back the veil on His wrath and gives us a look at the particular actions it births, "O LORD, rebuke me not in Your wrath, and chasten me not in Your burning anger." The two Hebrew words translated "wrath" and "anger" have the common connotation of a passionate displeasure about something. According to this verse, God acts in His passionate displeasure to "rebuke" and "chasten" sinners. We mustn't candy coat the meaning of these acts to alleviate their severity. We must openly admit their plain meaning that He inflicts harm on people, even King David here, who flaunt His word and will.

John clarifies what precipitates God's wrath in 3:36 of his gospel by linking it to people's posture toward Jesus, "He who believes in the Son has eternal life; but he who does not obey the Son will not see life, but the wrath of God abides on him." The tense of the word "abides" indicates that His wrath on those who reject Jesus doesn't come and go but is continually on them.

This statement hints at something that the Apostle Paul makes explicit in Ephesians 5:6, Colossians 3:6, and 1 Thessalonians 1:10 and that John confirms in Revelation

6:16-17. His wrath upon those who reject Jesus continues at His Second Coming and forever thereafter.

We conclude from this smattering of texts among the 600 that address the subject that the Bible doesn't share our diffidence in heralding God's wrath. It highlights it instead as an undeniable and non-negotiable aspect of His character.

God Is Wrathful Explained

Nonetheless, many Christians downplay God's wrath or even reject it altogether as a quality that's unworthy of Him. They do so for at least two reasons.

One is that they equate it with human wrath. "Wrath" is an old English word that *Dictionary.com* defines as "strong, stern, or fierce anger; deeply resentful indignation; ire." The definition is reflective of human anger since it's almost always laced with malice, self-righteousness, and pride. Because it is, it's a shameful quality that lets loose more detrimental consequences than we can predict, control, or retrieve. Many Christians perceive divine anger in that same way but since they know that God is utterly loving, good, and gracious, they proceed to draw the conclusion that it can't be part of His character.

Another reason they downplay or reject it is that they equate it with hell and think it's cruel. I visited a young man in jail who shattered a man's nose with a beer bottle for only slighting insulting him. Christians tend to view God's wrath as being like that, a cruel overreaction to the insult of sins. Since God is just and never overreacts, they reason, He cannot possess a wrath that consigns finite people to an everlasting hell.

Christians in either of those two camps are woefully misinformed. God's wrath, unlike human wrath, is righteous indignation, anger emptied of all malice, self-righteousness, and pride. We know that in terms of moral character, He's holy or 100% pure. Because He is, He always voluntarily reacts and responds adversely to sin. The Bible calls that adverse reaction and response of His "wrath."

We ourselves experience something like what He experiences. An acquaintance of mine learned that her neighbor was starving his outdoor dogs through sheer neglect. Possessing a sufficient degree of holiness or moral purity, she reacted inwardly when she did. She was disgusted and appalled. She also responded outwardly by calling the police who arrested him for cruelty to animals.

While that human reaction and response and others like it are a pale reflection of God's moral purity and its accompanying wrath, they do provide us at least a modicum of insight about it.

Possessing utter moral purity, He reacts adversely to sin by experiencing something that is like our feelings. The Bible employs several anthropopathisms (figurative language ascribing emotions to God) that denominate what those feelings are including "hate," "disgust," and "abomination." We can rightly say that sin appalls Him.

He doesn't just *react* adversely to sin; He *responds* adversely to it as well. He prohibited Moses from entering the Promised Land, inflicted leprosy on his sister Miriam, removed Saul from the throne, "struck" King David's son by Bathsheba, and paralyzed Jeroboam's hand to name a few Biblical examples. He acts to inflict harm on sinners, the specific nature of which is determined by the nature of the sin or sins they commit and the circumstances in which they commit them.

There is an ultimate harm He inflicts generally for the gravest of all sins, rejecting Jesus. It's what Paul calls in 2 Thessalonians 1:9 being "away from the presence of the Lord and from the glory of His power." His wrath cuts off rejecters of Jesus from Him and His kingdom so that they're unable to engage Him and it or to be engaged by Him or it. Consequently, they forfeit the foundational conditions of abundant life now. Monotony, poverty of soul, and pain not love, joy, and peace characterize their day-to-day lives on earth. They also forfeit perfection of life forever. Just as the love, joy, and peace of followers of Jesus is made full in heaven, so their monotony, poverty of soul, and pain are made full in hell. Jesus had this destiny of theirs in mind when He warned in Matthew 10:28 that God is "able to destroy both soul and body in hell." This destruction of body and soul that begins now and is made full at His Second Coming is the acutest manifestation of God's wrath.

As much as it may distress us to admit it, this wrath of His was at one time the fate of us all. Paul reminds us of just that in a hard hitting verse, Ephesians 2:3, "We too all . . . were by nature children of wrath, even as the rest." It's a popular notion in our current culture, both in ecclesiastical and secular circles, that no matter what our posture is toward Jesus, we're all children of God. The notion may be popular but it isn't Biblical. All of us at one time were children of wrath, objects of it, and if we aren't following Jesus, we still are.

But if we are following Jesus, we aren't because irony of all ironies God turned His wrath away from us and directed it toward, guess who, Himself. The Bible uses one word to convey this incredible reality in Romans 3:25, 1 John 2:2, 1 John 4:10, and Hebrews 2:17, "propitiation."

Propitiation is one of the Bible's cardinal tenets, connoting the pacifying of God's wrath by an offering. Because God is utterly just, His wrath will come against us because of our sins if it isn't rightly pacified. But there's only one way it can be. There must be an offering to Him that satisfies all the demands of His justice. And there is. That offering is Him.

It's here that Biblical religion is at variance with pagan religion. In pagan religion, people pacify the wrath of their many temperamental gods by giving them offerings. They follow the rule in doing so that the bigger the offering the more efficacious it is. The biggest offering of all is certainly a person's life, which explains the practice of human sacrifice. While we abhor this practice as irrational and cruel, we at the same time confess that pacifying divine wrath by an offering is part of both pagan and Biblical religion. But we also confess that the difference between the two overshadows the commonality they share. In paganism, propitiation is the work of man. His actions pacify the wrath of the gods. In Biblical religion, propitiation is the work of God Himself. His action pacified His wrath.

The Bible recounts what that action of His was. God the Son, Jesus, died on the cross for our sins. He took into Himself all of our sins and paid the penalty for them that we should have paid. That penalty was that Father God's wrath came against Him. He was cut off completely from Father God and His kingdom. He was, as a result, totally devoid of what had been His very essence – love, peace, and joy. We frequently hear people in a bad circumstance synopsize it by saying, "It's hell on earth." They're exaggerating as we know because there's only one person in history who literally went through hell on earth. That one person was Jesus on the cross when God's wrath came against Him as it will come against all rejecters of Him at His Second Coming.

That's the action God took and 1 John 4:10 reveals the result. Jesus was "the propitiation for our sins." Intrinsic to the word "propitiation" is the idea that God turned away His wrath from us by turning it on to Himself in the person of Jesus.

That He did so makes the crucifixion of Jesus a vivid historical demonstration and proof of God's wrath. It settles once and for all that He always voluntarily reacts and responds adversely to sins. He always detests sins and sooner or later, in one way or another, inflicts harm on sinners who don't repent.

God Is Wrathful Applied

The idea that a good and loving God "inflicts harm" is abhorrent to some but we need to muster up the courage to come to grips with the reality behind it. In *The Lion, the Witch, and the Wardrobe*, Mr. Beaver converses with Susan and Lucy about Aslan the lion who represents Jesus. When

Susan and Lucy ask him if Aslan is safe, Mr. Beaver replies, "'Course he isn't safe. But he's good."[42] His reply is spot on. God isn't malicious but He isn't safe either. We don't need a course in logic to deduce what the positive equivalent of "isn't safe" is. It's "dangerous" and no matter how distasteful the concept seems to us, He is!

He isn't dangerous in the abstract but dangerous as electricity, drunk drivers, pit bulls, inflation, debt, police, cancer, tornadoes, parents, worn out brakes, brown recluse spiders, and spoiled food are. Those things and God are dangerous because they can harm us and when the conditions are right, will.

Most of us have lived long enough to know how to effectively approach what is dangerous. We seek shelter in basements when tornados approach, turn the electricity off before changing a switch, replace brakes that are worn out, get colonoscopies after we're 50, and distance ourselves from pit bulls. We fear what is dangerous by expecting that it will harm us and acting so that it won't.

Jesus has this in mind when He directs us in Matthew 10:28, "Do not fear those who kill the body but are unable to kill the soul but rather fear Him who is able to destroy both soul and body in hell." He notes and correctly so that what the majority of us fear the most is what can damage or kill the body, like cancer or terrorists. But what we should fear the most is Him who can kill the soul and body in hell, God. We should expect that He can and will inflict immediate harms on us if we're at cross-purposes with Him and one day the ultimate of all harms, the ruination of our souls, and act so that He won't.

Fearing God, defined that way, may be foreign and even unsettling to you. If you're like me, you were taught to equate fearing Him with respecting and revering Him. I found respecting and revering Him much more palatable than expecting Him to harm me and so I, like many do, swallowed what I was taught hook, line, and sinker without any critical thought. But critical thought exposes the shallowness and error of what we were taught. There's no debating that we should respect and revere God but both responses are something apart from fearing Him. In nature, we fear Him as we fear anyone or anything that is dangerous. In degree, we fear Him far more.

And we're intelligent if we do. For centuries, at least since Aristotle, philosophers have attempted to pinpoint what intelligence is with neuroscientists recently entering the fray but they've reached no consensus. They've put forward numerous and varied pronouncements on the topic not one of which is as important and influential as the Bible's. It posits with absolute certitude that "The fear of the LORD is the beginning of wisdom" (Psalm 111:10; Proverbs 9:10) and that "The fear of the LORD is the beginning of knowledge" (Proverbs 1:7). Whatever intelligence is finally determined to be, it begins with fearing God, which necessarily means that it's "dumb" not to fear Him.

Our own personal experiences confirm this. Imagine a person hearing a tornado siren but not seeking shelter, replacing a light switch without turning the electricity off, driving 20 miles per hour over the speed limit in the presence of a police cruiser, and so on. An Arizona resident related to me that he never puts his shoes on in the morning without examining them first. He fears that a scorpion may have sought shelter in them during the night and will sting him if he puts them on. We know it from the happenings of real life like that one. It's intelligent to fear some things and dumb not to. Discerning the fundamental nature or order of some things, we expect that they will harm us in one way or another. We then act so that they won't. That is intelligence.

And it begins with fearing God. The word "beginning" doesn't mean "first" as in a stage that we eventually leave behind for a second stage. It means first as in dominant or controlling. The dominant or controlling principle when it comes to intelligence is to fear God. It's the most intelligent thing a human can do. A law school professor teaching our Trial Techniques class offered a practical piece of advice he advised us to follow when we became attorneys: "Always remember that the courtroom is the judge's and his word is law. So fear him as you would a 600 pound gorilla and do what he says." We should have the same posture toward God that attorneys have toward judges. The universe is His and His word is law. He isn't malicious but He is wrathful and dangerous. So fear Him! It's the beginning of intelligence.

CHAPTER 17

"ALWAYS IN CHARACTER"

God Is Righteous/Just

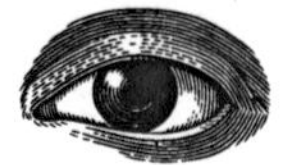

It's a vital question that behavioral professionals from psychologists to life coaches devote themselves to answering. Why do people do the things they do? But there's another even more vital question that all of us need to devote ourselves to answering. Why does God do the things He does? It's because He's righteous and just.

God Is Righteous and Just Revealed

The righteousness and justice of God hold a prominent but confusing place in the Bible. I say "confusing" because our English Bibles translate one set of Hebrew words (Old Testament) and one set of Greek words (New Testament) with two sets of English words – right, righteous, and righteousness on the one hand and just, justice, and justify on the other. Sometimes, the translators render the Hebrew or Greek word groups as one of the "right" word groups and other times as one of the "just" word groups. However they render them, the commonality, as the following texts show, is that all the words relate to actions of God.

I begin with the "right" word group translations.

Ezra 9:15 uses a statement of substance to espouse God's righteousness, "O LORD God of Israel, You are righteous." It relates this attribute of His to Him punishing the Israelites "less than our iniquities deserve" and giving them "an escaped remnant" (verse 13).

Jeremiah queries how God's righteousness works itself out in a world where the wicked prosper as the godly suffer. With the enmity his countrymen at Anathoth showed him fresh in his mind, he brings a complaint against God in 12:1 of his prophetic book, "Righteous are You, O LORD, that I would plead my case with You; indeed I would discuss matters of justice with you." Jeremiah questions God's righteousness in the face of the wicked prospering even as they're dealing treacherously with the godly like him. Further inquiry convinces him that God always acts as He should, in this case bearing patiently with the wicked so that they might come to repentance.

But that doesn't mean the wicked should presume on His patience precisely because He is righteous and thus, won't always act patiently toward them. Referring to the seven bowls of wrath and the judgments on the wicked that accompany them, the angel cries out in Revelation 16:5, "Righteous are You, who are and who were, O Holy One, because you judged these things." Notice that God is righteous both in bearing with the wicked and in punishing them.

The same Hebrew word and Greek word translated "righteous" and "righteousness" in the preceding New American Standard Bible texts are translated "just" and "justice" in others.

In Nehemiah 9, the repatriated Levites place the long history of their nation Israel in the context of God's greatness, pointing out in verse 33, "However, You are just in all that has come upon us; for you have dealt faithfully." By their own admission, God's treatment of them is faithful or as it should be because He's just.

The prophet Zechariah assigns this same attribute to the coming Messiah, Jesus, in 9:9 of the book that bears his name, "Behold, your king is coming to you; He is just and endowed with salvation." Messiah, he prophesies, will achieve salvation for humankind in a way that's consistent with the character of God.

Paul elaborates on how He did so in Romans 3:21-26. Highlighting God's righteousness in verses 21, 22, 25, and 26, he proceeds to single out its primary manifestation in verse 26. He's "just and the justifier of the one who has faith in Jesus." Being both just and justifier means that He punishes sinners for their sins and at the same time regards and treats them as if they were sinless.

We deduce from these texts and others like them that the righteousness and justness of God are separate realities but so closely related that it takes precision to distinguish between them.

God Is Righteous and Just Explained

So let's be precise. That God is righteous means that He always acts according to His nature unaffected by anyone or anything outside of Him. What He thinks, feels, and does always comes out of and is always consistent with the perfectly unified working together of all of His attributes.

Perhaps the best way to explain it is by comparing it to a curious but revealing human phenomenon. If you're like me, you're struck by the scandalous behavior of public figures and the meme to which they often resort to minimize the tarnishing of their reputation, "I acted out of character." What they're saying is that it isn't "like" them to do what they did. They're urging us to believe that they're better people than their behavior shows them to be.

Their meme suggests that all of us act out of character here and there due to the pressures of life and many behavioral professionals agree. But others and I disagree. Absent organic issues that override it, we believe that others and we always act within the bounds of our character or nature. It's always "like" us to do what we do. If we act recklessly because of the strain of a particular circumstance, it's because we're the kind of person who acts that way in that circumstance.

Whether or not people act out of character may be open to be debate. But whether or not God does isn't. He never acts out of character. It's always "like" Him to do what He does. He is always "true" to Himself. More precisely, all of His attributes and only them, always working perfectly together, always fully direct the divine thoughts, feelings, and behaviors that flow from them. Every single thought and feeling God has and every single action He takes "jibes" with the harmonious interaction of all of His attributes. And since all of His attributes are perfect, so are all of His thoughts, feelings, and actions. He's righteous in other words.

This righteousness of His extends to all of His dealings with humans. He always acts upon them and interacts with them consistently with all of His attributes, including His holiness and love. And it's that particularly to what the word "just" refers.

The action of divine justness is judgment. God assesses the nature of what humans think, feel, and do. He then gives them what we call their "just deserts" for thinking, feeling, and doing it. He punishes or rewards them accordingly. His judgments are always fully informed and perfectly fair so that He always rewards or punishes humans in a way that's finally consistent with His holiness and love, even if it seems immediately inconsistent. Or to say it another way, He always does right by Himself and us, in that order of importance, when He judges us.

He doing so is no small task because His love on the one hand and His holiness on the other contain what we might call contending mandates. Those mandates in turn posed an unimagined and very real moral dilemma for Him. In the movie *The Dark Knight*, Batman's enemy the Joker creates a series of moral conundrums for him to solve in order to reveal the animal nature of man. Batman must expose his true identity or the Joker will kill one person every day. He must rescue either Rachel his true love or Dent the righteous hope of the city. And he must save a boatload of citizens or a boatload of convicts. As gut wrenching as those moral dilemmas are, not one or even all in combination come close to matching the difficulty and consequence of the one God faced.

Paul delves into the nub of this divine dilemma in the text I mentioned earlier, Romans 3:21-26. As he articulates it in verse 26, how can God be "just" and yet "justifier of the one who has faith in Jesus"? The dilemma arises from what appears to be the opposing mandates of His love and holiness. Because He loves us, He desires to pardon us for our sins and to give us what we don't deserve, spiritual life now and forever. In contrast, because He's holy, He desires to punish us for our sins and give us what we do deserve, spiritual death now and forever. God being righteous means that He acts consistently with His love and pardons us and with His holiness and punishes us. But how can He do both? How can He satisfy His love without thwarting His holiness and satisfy His holiness without thwarting His love?

That's the moral dilemma God faced and Paul reveals in Romans 3 how He solved it. All who have "faith in Jesus Christ," verse 22, are "justified as a gift by His grace," verse 24. The Greek word translated "justified" is a legal term that connotes pardon, in this context pardon for our sins. According to verse 25, God achieved it by displaying Jesus publicly on the cross, which was a "demonstration of His righteousness," verse 26. We might present this idea of Paul's more forcefully by declaring that the death of Jesus is the historical showcase of God's righteousness, an act that satisfied all the mandates of both His love and holiness as no other ever has or will. It did so because of what He became on the cross.

Weknowtheanswer.com is a website that searches and collects answers to questions it posts. One it posted in 2017 affronted many of its respondents whose answers took the website to task for its gall in even asking it, "Jesus Christ was the most evil man to ever live?"[43] As distasteful as many considered the question to be, it intimates, unintentionally I'm sure, a profound conclusion about Jesus that only the most thoughtful among us would draw.

Suppose you were asked to name the most evil person who ever lived. Who would it be? Adolph Hitler perhaps or maybe Joseph Stalin or Pol Pot. But there's One who was more evil than any of those or all of those in combination. That One was Jesus during the six hours He hung on the cross because He hung there as the substitute for every person who ever has lived and ever will.

Peter's asservation in 1 Peter 2:24 illumines the substitutionary nature of Jesus' death experience, "He Himself bore our sins in His body on the cross."

It's unmistakable that during His six hours on the cross He stood in for us by taking all our sins and everyone else's into Himself. Think of an unimaginably self-centered sin such as an unfaithful husband giving his unsuspecting wife the HIV virus he knew he had. As far as Father God was concerned, it was as if Jesus Himself had done that and every other sinful act. He was the worst murderer, adulterer, gossip, slanderer, materialist, narcissist, and so on who ever lived and Father God judged and punished Him as if He were.

In doing so, He solved the moral dilemma He faced. He resolved the conflicting mandates of His love and holiness by standing in for us in the person of Jesus. He didn't allay His judgment or condemnation of sin but let it fall on Him instead. He could as a result do what His love directed Him to do, pardon us, without compromising what His holiness directed Him to do, punish us. Or as Paul wrote, He could be just and the justifier of those who have faith in Jesus. He's righteous, always in character, in this way and in all ways.

God Is Righteous and Just Applied

Most of us would admit, in our moments of candor at least, that there are times when we aren't so sure of that and we're in the good company of the psalmists when we aren't. A recurring theme in the Psalter is the questioning of God's rectitude in dealing with the wicked who are prospering and the righteous who are suffering and the conflicted spirit that springs from it.

Asaph, founder of one of the temple choirs, wrestles with this distressing issue in his eye-opening Psalm 73. Envious because the wicked are prospering and the righteous, including him, are suffering, he expresses his grievances in verses 1-14 about the righteousness of God's dealings. They overwhelm him, giving full release to the self-pity and the misdirected conclusion of verse 13 that there's no benefit to being godly and pure. His experience is representative of the strain that doubts about God's fairness place on our relationship with Him.

This is after all a natural relational phenomenon. J.M. Barrie touches on it in his celebrated novel *Peter Pan*. What transpired after Peter gave Hook a fighting chance in their duel was as follows: "It was then that Hook bit him. Not the pain of this but its unfairness was what dazed Peter. It made him quite helpless. He could only stare horrified. Every child is affected thus the first time he is treated unfairly. All he thinks he has a right to when he comes to you to be yours is fairness. After you have been unfair to him he will love you again, but he will never afterwards be quite the same boy. No one ever gets over the first unfairness; no one except Peter."[44] Barrie portrays the vigorous and detrimental impact unfairness has on people and their relationships and he's correct in doing so.

They include God's people in their relationship with Him. Whether we're conscious of the logical thought process behind it or not, we must be convinced that God is just or fair in all His dealings with us in order to love Him. If someone is unfair to us, we know it's because he or she is either incompetent or bad or both. Incompetence and badness by their very nature inject uneasiness and even fear into relationships that make abandoned self-giving love demanding at best and impossible at worst.

Relationship with God is no exception. If we perceive unfairness in either the personal traits He bestows upon us or the life circumstances into which He brings us or allows us to be brought, we'll be too uncertain in our relationship with Him to love Him. As Aspah's response in Psalm 73:13 demonstrates, we'll likely resent Him instead. Perceived unfairness is a fly in the ointment of any relationship including ours with God that can and will, if it continues, eventually ruin it.

I'd quickly note here that there's plenty of that, the perceived unfairness of God, to go around. I've already referenced the legendary struggle the psalmists had with the wicked prospering and the righteous suffering and they aren't alone. I'll never forget the embittered words of a Christian mother I counseled who had a schizophrenic son: "My agnostic neighbors have three healthy children but my husband and I are going through hell on earth with our son. Where's the justice in that?" It's a valid question that reverberates over and over again in the psalms and normal human experience.

The issue of God's justness though reaches well beyond the wicked prospering and the righteous suffering to the most commonplace disparities readily observable in the persons and circumstances of day-to-day life. You undoubtedly know what they are because you've wrestled with them or at least wondered about them I'm sure. Some of us came from good homes with parents who loved us; others of us came from bad homes with parents who neglected or abused us. Some of us have high IQ's; others of us have average or low IQ's. Some of us have consistently good health; others of us have consistently bad health. Some of us are exceedingly talented; others of us are typically talented. Some of us live in cultural contexts of freedom; others of us live in cultural contexts of oppression. These disparities and many others like them incite envy and the resulting disappointment with God that grips even long time Christians today.

As we'd expect, disappointment with God destabilizes or even extinguishes our relationship with Him. We mustn't sweep our disappointment in Him, if we have it, under the rug by ignoring or denying it. To be able to love Him and to let Him love us, we must "fess up" and eliminate it as a factor in our spiritual and psychological lives.

One of the ways we can do so is by revisiting Psalm 73 and learning from Asaph what he learned.

His forthright and courageous admission in verse 22 unmasks the active agents behind the disappointment with God to which perceived injustices give birth. They are envy and complaint. It also pictures what envy and complaint do to us, "Then I was senseless and ignorant; I was like a beast before you." Those active agents blind us to the controlling realities about our persons and lives that trump the disparities that we so clearly see. According to Asaph, we can be and often are as ignorant of those controlling realities as a beast or animal is.

Implicit in Asaph's admission in verse 22 is an effective strategy for dealing with our disappointment with God. It's to "get real." It's to identify and define the controlling realities about our persons and lives. We find when we do that while the disparities of life make a difference, the controlling realities are decisive. Taking only the disparities into account leads us to logically conclude God's unjust. In contrast, taking the controlling realities into account leads us to logically conclude He's just. It isn't those who believe God is just who have their heads buried in the sand. It's those who believe He isn't who do. So let's get our heads out of the sand and see the controlling realities.

Asaph draws our attention to one of those in verses 17-20. He relates here that his whole outlook changed when "I perceived their end," verse 17. He's referring to what the fate of the prospering wicked will be on Judgment Day. According to verse 20, it's that God "will despise their form." The word "despise" is laden with the pathos of their destiny, several details of which C.S. Lewis unfolds in his famous sermon "The Weight of Glory." They will be "repelled, exiled, estranged, and unspeakably ignored."[45] It's an ignominious end that puts their temporal prosperity in the larger context of eternity and lays to rest any wonderings we may have about the equity of it. It's an end that, if we understand and believe it, makes us grieved for the wicked not envious of them.

Asaph opens our eyes to another controlling reality in verse 24. Unlike the New Testament with its pericopes (paragraphs of thought) and developed doctrine, the Old Testament offers only a few flashes of insight here and there about life after death. Verse 24 is one of those, giving us a glimpse into the ultimate end of the righteous who are suffering, "With Your counsel You will guide me, and afterward receive me to glory." The word "glory" stands in sharp contrast to the word "despise" in verse 20. The eternal destiny of the righteous is as glorious as that of the wicked is ignoble.

Because it is, placing the righteous in the context of eternity goes a long way toward soothing if not curing the sense of injustice we feel about their suffering. It takes the sting out. Paul intends his cursory comment on the subject in 2 Corinthians 4:17 to do just that, "For momentary, light affliction is producing for us an eternal weight of glory far beyond all comparison." Saint Teresa of Avila took this principle and clothed it in terms to which even the simplest among us can relate, "In light of heaven, the worst suffering on earth will be seen to be no more serious than one night in an inconvenient hotel."[46] Keep in mind that she was no theoretician drawing conclusions like that one while sitting in the confines of her ivory tower. She witnessed and participated in more suffering than most of us will and yet, in the midst of it all, saw a just God who will ultimately make every wrong right.

But God's justness doesn't operate only in the life the wicked and righteous will live. It operates in the life they're living right now in their day-to-day worlds. Asaph puts his finger on what is perhaps the decisive of all controlling realities in verse 28, "But as for me, the nearness of God is my good."

Think about your life in daily terms, the 18 hours from the time you arise in the morning until the time you go to bed at night. All of us hope for the best, the greatest goods, during those hours and attempt to embrace and experience them: delicious meals, a job well done at work, invigorating exercise, enjoyable entertainment, and satisfying experiences with family or friends to name a few. But according to Asaph in verse 28, the chief good, the most joy-producing by far, is engaging God and being engaged by Him. The joy of experiencing Him personally that way in the moments that make up our days dwarfs the joy of experiencing any other good. I'm not embellishing for the sake of effect in using the word "dwarfs." The truth is that to have every other good but not to have God is to have nothing, and to have no other good but to have God is to have everything.

A preacher told about an itinerant nationalist missionary who owned nothing except the belongings in his backpack. Yet, the preacher observed he was the most joyful person he ever met. Why? It's because he had God and to have God is to have everything.

That's the truth and the justness of God shines through it because the righteous even in their suffering have him and the wicked in their prosperity don't. Pursuant to the principle I just shared, therefore, the righteous have "everything" and the wicked have "nothing."

But it isn't just righteousness and wickedness that come into play here. It's the disparities of life as well. Verse 23's "nearness of God" levels the playing field because it's available equally to anyone who wants and chooses it. Those who came from good homes and those who came from bad ones, those with high IQ's and those with average or low IQ's, those with good health and those with bad health, and so on can act upon God and be acted upon by Him. Each one then experiences a resulting joy that's equal in its degree and effect upon them. Those who experience this joy, irrespective of how little or much they have going for them, would happily shout it from the rooftops if they could. God is just.

But as we've learned in this chapter, He's more than that. God is just because He's righteous and it's in His righteousness that we rest assured. You and I can lay our heads on our pillows at night and sleep like a baby because He's always "in character." He always acts like the utterly lovely and utterly competent being He is.

CHAPTER 18

"SURPRISE"

God Is Joyful

Chapter 18 is the point of our arrival, coming to the last of God's attributes that I'll attend to with the caveat that I'm not "saving the best for last." As we've learned in Chapters 3-17, all of His attributes are equally grand. What I am doing is saving the least known for last.

A skeptical attorney and I were conversing before a pretrial when the subject of God came up. Responding to a comment I made about Him, he stated definitively where he stood. "God is a cosmic bore," he said.

Many of us wouldn't know how to respond to that accusation of his. Because "cosmic bore" is patently derogatory, we would be appalled and vehemently deny it. But we'd leave it at that because what He is in contradistinction to boring is so rarely explained or even mentioned that we don't know it. I personally have never heard a pastor or teacher broach the subject in passing let alone descend into its depths.

So, I'm broaching it now. I ask you, if God isn't boring, what is He? If you're as uninformed as I was for much of my life, the answer may surprise you. He's joyful.

God Is Joyful Revealed

While preachers and teachers at large are generally silent about the joyfulness of God, the Bible isn't. Its express teachings about this attribute of His are not as voluminous as they are of others but they are coherent enough to inform and inspire us.

Paul uses a curious epithet of God in 1 Timothy 1:11 and 6:15 that is a fitting introduction to His joyfulness. He calls Him "the blessed God." The Greek word translated blessed is the same that Jesus uses in the Beatitudes in Matthew 5:3-12 to describe the condition of those who access Jesus and His kingdom at hand. Some English Bibles translate it "happy" but "blessed" is closer to the condition that it's intended to describe, an ongoing and life-enveloping joy. Kingdom people are blessed in that sense and as Paul's epithet intimates, so is God. Blessedness or joyfulness characterizes every aspect of His being.

Isaiah 62:5 uses a strong metaphor that underscores the vim and vigor of God's joyfulness, "And as the bridegroom rejoices over the bride, so your God will rejoice over you." Assuming that His experience of us, the spiritual Israel, is a continuation of His experience of the national Israel, it's like that of a groom on His wedding day. Most of us who were grooms remember the unadulterated joyfulness of our wedding day that according to Proverbs 5:18 can and hopefully does persist even now in our marital lives. This greatest of all relational joys is only a pale reflection of God's.

When everything is said and done though, the joyfulness of God is fully displayed in Jesus. It's a cardinal principle of the Christian faith that Jesus shows us God. What Jesus is like the Father and Holy Spirit are like as well. He Himself delineates what He and consequently they are like in His Last Supper Discourse. In John 15:11, He relates to His disciples why He taught them what He did, "so that My joy may be in you, and that your joy may be made full." He reiterates that same condition and aspiration of His in His high priestly prayer for His disciples of all generations. He asks Father God in John 17:13 that "they may have My joy made full in themselves."

The word "full" in both texts denotes the extent of the divine joy. God couldn't possess any more of it than He does. He's perfect and limitless in it just as He is in His other attributes. He's utterly joyful in other words so that His joy exceeds ours to the same extent that His power, knowledge, and love, for instance, exceed ours. We can rightly infer from that fact about Him what Pastor Joe Wittwer does: "Friends, that's pretty good theology! I want to convince you that God is the most joyful person in the universe! The God I wish you knew is joyful!"[47]

In the movie *Pollyanna*, the protagonist Polyanna mentions to a stern preacher whose sermons are always gloom and doom what she calls "the happy texts," ones that call us to rejoice and be glad. She went on to say that the Bible contains 360 such texts and she was approximately right, one for each day of the year. The Bible is a joyful book because its author, God, is an utterly joyful being.

God Is Joyful Explained

It's one thing to know that God is joyful but an entirely different thing to know what it means that He is. We face the same challenge in defining God's joy that we do each of His other attributes. We can only think and speak of it anthropopathically because it's beyond anything we've ever experienced or can comprehend as finite creatures.

Paul's 1 Timothy 1:11 and 6:15 texts are, I believe, the best place to start in our attempt to process what it means. Admittedly, commentators conjecture about what Paul intends the word "blessed" to connote about God but I favor its conventional meaning. God experiences beatitude. A common definition of beatitude is "ecstasy or bliss," words that we can accurately apply to Him and that constitute His joy. This joy doesn't refer to an emotional tone but rather a permanent condition or state of being ecstatic or blissful that has accompanying emotional tones, and again I'm speaking figuratively. Those emotional tones include happiness, hilarity, enthusiasm, passion, and delight, all of which are rooted in His condition of joy.

Keeping in mind that Jesus shows us God enhances our comprehension of God's joy and the emotional tones that spring from it. We can be certain that Jesus wasn't the slow moving, slowing talking, stuffed shirt that so many movies make Him out to be. We can't deny He was what Isaiah 53 calls "a man of sorrows" who was grieved over the broken condition of the world and people around Him. But at the same time, He was an enthusiast who reveled in the countless wonders of the people and world around Him. He "sucked the marrow out of life" to quote poet Henry David Thoreau, a trait of His that likely elicited John the Baptist's questions about Him in Matthew 11 and the Pharisees' criticism of Him in Luke 7 that He was a glutton and drunk. People had never seen anyone as joyful as He was and couldn't quite come to grips with it. As He Himself said it in the John 15:11 and 17:13 texts, His joy was "full." And so are the Father's and the Holy Spirit's, making the triune God "the most joyful person" or more accurately since He's three persons, the most joyful "being" in the universe.

One of the most creative and humorous writers of the 20th century, G.K. Chesterton, peeled off a layer of God's joy that uncovers its richness and depth: "Because children have abounding vitality, because they are in spirit fierce and free, therefore they want things repeated and unchanged. They always say, 'Do it again'; and the grown-up person does it again until he is nearly dead. For grown-up people are not strong enough to exalt in monotony. But perhaps God is strong enough to exalt in monotony. It is possible that God says every morning, "Do it again' to the sun; and every evening, 'Do it again' to the moon. It may be that He has the eternal appetite of infancy; for we have sinned and grown old, and Father is younger than we are."[48] Chesterton's reflections here are a memorable and ironic "take" on the divine joy. It's splendorous enough to exalt in monotony with the practical consequence that there is no monotony in the experience of God. He has the eternal appetite of infancy that exalts in all things great and small. He's utterly joyful.

And so is His life. Some of us have never entertained the thought that God has a life but He does and what a mind boggling one it is.

In Job 39:13-18, He pulls back the veil and gives us a glimpse into this life of His. These verses are part of a divine discourse in Chapters 39-40 that puts God in His place as Sovereign and Job in his as servant by underlining His wisdom and power as displayed in particular creations of nature. One of those, in 39:13-18, is the ostrich.

Let's be honest and come right out and say it about the ostrich. It's weird. Forgetting for a moment that it's a bird (does it look like a bird to you) and that it can't fly, let's focus on the oddities that God does in His description of it. Verse 13: It's the poster child for "You're so ugly" jokes and behaves as strangely as it looks, the male's uproarious ritual of courtship, wildly flapping his wings, a classic case in point. Verses 14-16: The female won't be getting a "Mother of the Year" award any time soon. Forgetting that her eggs and young are there, she's oblivious to the dangers they face not just from other beasts but her own ungainliness itself. Verses 17-18: Female or male, it isn't the "brightest bulb in the pack" of the animal kingdom. The ancient Arabs coined a proverb, "Stupid as an ostrich" that only reinforces God's admission here that He "has made her forget wisdom, and has not given her a share of understanding." Since God Himself created it, His comments are the "last word" on the ostrich. It's ugly, eccentric, clumsy, and dumb.

God's hilarity in describing the ostrich in Job 39:13-18 is, I believe, intentional and purposes to convey to us why He created it the way He did. It was for His entertainment and ours. The ostrich is one of His stand-up comedians in nature outclassing the funniest human stand up comedians in the business. We get a kick out of the ostrich and I don't think it's demeaning of God to say that He does too but even more so, which was why He made it in the first place.

Bound up in His experience of the ostrich is a God-fact to which few Christians have ever given any passing thought let alone deliberation. He has a life. One of the best loved shows in the Age of Television was the popular *This Is Your Life*. We could produce just such a show for God because He truly does have a life that in its totality makes the most breathless moments of ours seem boring in comparison.

John Piper preached a sermon about creation revealing the glory of God and told about spending a night in a beach side motel on the ocean. This motel, he stated with a tone of incredulity, also had a swimming pool. And when he looked out from the balcony of his room, he went on to say with a gleam in his eye, this was what he saw, "Man's pool and God's pool." The ocean is just that, God's pool. In terms of experience, it is to Him what a swimming pool or even a fish tank is to us. Most of us have seen pictures of the breath-taking landscapes in the depths of the ocean and the fantastic creatures that inhabit it. Imagine the thrill of experiencing all of those landscapes and creatures from every possible angle and point of view. What we can only imagine God experiences and revels in doing so.

Taking in oceans is just the tip of the iceberg in God's life, if even that. All of us have had thrilling and sometimes even breathtaking experiences of a phenomenon of nature, a human invention, a game, a hobby, a breakthrough achievement, a desire or need meeting serendipity, and much more. His experiences of those things were comprehensive to the max and thus richer, deeper, and fuller than we can even begin to envisage. We are sometimes awash in an undulation of joy producing emotions, which are only a portent of those that continually flood His being.

That's the life of God and contrary to the opinion of some the idea that He has one isn't beneath Him and doesn't denigrate Him. God is no stern cosmic stuffed shirt or even a detached and disinterested creator. Quite the opposite, He unceasingly experiences happiness, hilarity, enthusiasm, passion, and delight as He cares for and interacts with all of His creation whether it's an angel, a human, a black hole, or an ostrich. He is an utterly joyful being with a life that's the same, utterly joyful.

God Is Joyful Applied

No other attributes of God speak more urgently to those of us who love and follow Him than this one does.

In his celebrated novel *A Portrait of the Artist as a Young Man,* James Joyce explains his hero's decision not to become a priest. He was afraid that his face would become like the faces of the religious people he knew: "A mirthless mask reflecting a sunken day . . . sourfavored and devout, shot with pink tinges of suffocated anger."[49] I wonder. Is that what you and I see when we look in the mirror, "a mirthless mask reflecting a sunken day?" For some of us who follow Jesus, the answer is "Yes, that's what we see."

We need to be honest here and own up to it that some if not many who follow Jesus aren't exactly models of joy. One of the reasons they aren't lies in their conception of holiness. Specifically, they connect holiness with gloominess. They've somehow acquired the belief that sanctified people are solemn people and so, have become that. They've shut joy and celebration out of their lives with the effect that they're stuffy, stodgy, and stiff.

Jesus, however, destroyed the myth of Christian gloominess by modeling and teaching joy. As we've already learned in John 15:11 and 17:13, His joy that was demonstrated in the totality of His life was "full" or perfect. He was an exuberant person whose everyday life exuded laughter, humor, and play.

And we can be too. He made it plain in John 15:11 that we can in this fallen world of ours have a large measure of the joy and its accompanying emotional tones that He had and will if we follow Him. As we follow Him, we become increasingly like Him, and as we become increasingly like Him, we become increasingly joyful. This Jesus-joy of ours then continues into our life after life on earth. As C.S. Lewis rightly remarked, "Joy is the serious business of heaven."[50] God created us to be joyful, in other words, and intends that joy to be a defining mark of the kingdom life now and forever.

Joy's place in the kingdom life now is that of a necessity not a luxury and we can't do without it. Nehemiah's admonition to the Israelites in Nehemiah 8:10 bears this out, "The joy of the LORD is your strength." The context of his admonition, the Jewish people mourning their sins, enables us to define with precision the kind of strength to which he's alluding. It's spiritual strength. Think of it as joy being a line of defense against sin.[51] The presence of joy and its accompanying emotional tones weakens the power of temptation by making sin seem uninviting to us. In contrast, the absence of it strengthens the power of temptation by making sin seem inviting to us. Practically speaking then, fullness of joy supports holiness of life with its efforts to do what is good and right while deficiency of joy undermines it. No one is more vulnerable to the attacks of Satan and temptation than joyless Christians. No one is more invulnerable to them than joyful Christians. Joyless Christians are Satan's dream; joyful Christians are his nightmare.

Joy is no take it or leave it proposition in our lives with God. It's absolutely indispensable.

The first step in achieving Jesus-joy is to apprentice ourselves to Him. We firmly make the decision to be with Him in order to become like Him and to learn and do all that He says. We then arrange all of our everyday affairs around carrying out that decision. The Holy Spirit works in us as we do to increasingly produce Jesus-joy in us as one of what Paul calls His "fruit" in Galatians 5:22. It's a condition or state that gives birth to emotional tones like happiness, passion, enthusiasm, wonder, and delight.

But while this condition or state is primarily the work of the Holy Spirit, it isn't only His. We must open ourselves up to His joy-producing activity in us by practicing related spiritual disciplines. Some scoff at the proposition that these are spiritual disciplines but they are if we do them unto the Lord and as He would do them if He were us.

First, we laugh. We're able to because we're in the image of God and He Himself experiences something like laughter. It's part of His joy. Bruce Marchiano claims that Jesus "smiled wider and laughed heartier than any human being who has ever walked the planet." He's right and if we desire to be like Jesus, we'll laugh too. In Psalm 126:2, the psalmist writes about God breaking through to bless Israel, "Then our mouth was filled with laughter and our tongue with joyful shouting." When we're blessed by our encounters and experiences with Jesus and His kingdom at hand, we can and should laugh. His best and brightest friends through the centuries such as Charles Spurgeon, G.K. Chesterton, and C.S. Lewis grasped this and acted accordingly. Laughter was a constant backdrop of their lives and experiences. Spurgeon, for instance, said that laughter was his favorite sound and often roared with it from the pulpit. Let's quit taking ourselves so seriously, lighten up, and laugh.

Another spiritual discipline that opens us up to the Holy Spirit's joy producing work is play or having fun. Eugene Peterson wrote a book titled *Christ Plays in Ten Thousand Places* and that's right. He does and so do the Father and the Holy Spirit. God plays and we should too. Play is nothing more than having fun in a host and variety of ways like eating, telling stories, playing games, reading, writing, using language, and playing with toys to name a few. John Wesley said that the one who plays when he's a child will play when he's a man, reflecting his belief that adults should play. I'm not embellishing when I contend that it's essential to our spiritual and psychological health that we do.

In *The Screwtape Letters* of C.S. Lewis, the leader demon Screwtape teaches his underling demon Wormwood that humans having fun hinders Satan's cause: "Fun is closely related to joy – arising from the play instinct . . . In itself it has wholly undesirable tendencies; it promotes charity, courage, contentment, and many other evils."[52] It's a simple point. Play assists in our spiritual and moral development and the creation of joy.

A third spiritual discipline that the Holy Spirit uses to create Jesus-joy in us is joking around. Jokes are about the incongruities, oddities, and superficial sufferings of life. To joke around means to recognize, appreciate, verbalize, and act on those. People, for instance, seem to think pastors have a lot of stress, prompting a parishioner to give me an "Anti-stress Kit." It's a large circle on a sheet of paper with the words "Bang Head Here" on the circle. Underneath are three instructions: (1) "Place on firm surface"; (2) "Follow direction on circle"; and (3) "Repeat until stress is gone or you are unconscious." The parishioner and I had a good laugh together, reflecting and developing, even if slightly, the relationship between us. Joking around is a vital component of koinonia or fellowship and a catalyst to communal joy. You may have observed that joking around and the laughter that follows it are two of the first things to go when people are in conflict with each other. That's because it's a critical component of the koinonia that the Holy Spirit wants to generate and the joy that's inherent in it.

As incredulous as it may seem to you, laughing, playing, and joking are spiritual disciplines if we do them unto the Lord and as He would do them if He were us. They provide the Holy Spirit with the fertile ground He needs to create the condition of Jesus-joy in us, making us the God-pleasing persons He wants us to be.

Notice I said "God-pleasing." I'm reminded of something Martin Luther said in that vein: "It is pleasing to the dear God whenever thou rejoicest or laughest from the bottom of thy heart." He was right. It is pleasing and it's no longer a surprise to us why it is. It's because God is the most joyful being in the universe!

CHAPTER 19

"FIRST THINGS FIRST"

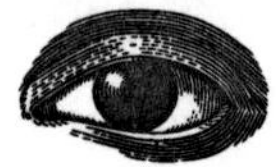

"Now what?" A middle-aged businessman had just "gone forward to the altar" after a worship service to publicly declare his decision to be a disciple of Jesus. After several elders and I finished praying for him, he looked up at us and asked, "Now what? What do I do?" It was a welcome question that assured us he was sincere about the decision he made. It was also a pressing question because our answer to it would to a large extent direct the course and nature of his discipleship. The "Now what?" question is one that all of us who have taken up with Jesus need to thoughtfully answer for our own sake and the sake of others we might have the privilege to counsel.

A well-worn axiom should guide our answer to it. The axiom is "first things first." There is normally a sequential order of things that must be followed in order to successfully accomplish the particular goal before us. To put first things first means to get our ducks in a row – to recognize and follow that sequential order.

For the disciple of Jesus, the goal before him or her is to have what Thomas a Kempis called a "familiar friendship" with God. It's to have an ongoing interactive relationship with Him that unceasingly deepens and grows. This relationship is the lynchpin of all the activities, events, principles, and truths of Christianity and the ultimate prize of discipleship to Jesus. And there is in our pursuit of it a "first thing first."

Years ago, a father and mother approached me and asked me to "talk some sense" into their 21 year-old daughter who had just gotten engaged. They claimed that her fiancé was a manipulative, impulsive, and irresponsible slacker who was "no good" for their daughter. Several days later, I spoke to the daughter whose retort was that her parents were being unreasonable and unfair in judging her fiancé. She went on to rave about him that he was a creative, carefree, and affirming spirit who loved life and inspired her to do the same. As she left my office that day, I mused that one wouldn't know that her parents and she were talking about the same young man.

It was an eye-opening experience from which I gleaned two life-lessons. First, all of us have a vision of the people with whom we're acquainted. We perceive them to possess certain qualities or traits that they may or may not possess. And second, the vision we have of them determines how we relate to them.

We draw from those life-lessons the valid conclusion that vision is the foundation upon which individual relationships are built. How we perceive people shapes how we feel about them and how we act upon and interact with them.

But it isn't just people is it? It's God as well. Our vision of Him truly is the basis of our relationship with Him. How we perceive Him governs how we relate to Him. It dictates how we feel about Him and respond to Him. That necessarily means that the sufficiency or insufficiency of our response to Him is determined by the sufficiency or insufficiency of our vision of Him.

The Bible does spell out what the sufficiency of response to God is. Pulling a host of Old Testament and New Testament texts together, we learn that we should love, fear, trust, obey, and serve Him. Those are what I would call the "elemental postures" toward God that develop and deepen as we carry out our discipleship to Jesus and that comprise our part of relationship with Him. But those postures are possible only if we have a vision of Him that supports them.

Much of the frustration and disappointment that Christians feel stems from the failure of Christian leaders to comprehend and publish this basic truism. Pastors, for instance, constantly chide us in their sermons to love, fear, trust, obey, or serve God but leave it at that, implying that we can do so directly and instantaneously by deciding to. But we can't. We can't just decide to do those things and immediately do it, which makes us frustrated and disappointed when we try.

Those elemental responses to God are what Dallas Willard called "indirect freedoms." They're "freedoms" in that we can do them but they're "indirect" in that we have to do others things first that change us in one way or the other before we can. With regard to the elemental responses to God, the first of those other things is to know Him. We cannot love Him, fear Him, trust Him, obey, and serve Him (habitually at least) until we first of all know Him. As hard as we may try, there's no short cut that gets us around this sequence.

Philosophers of various eras including John Grote, William James, and Bertrand Russell have distinguished between two kinds of knowledge. One is knowledge by description, which is knowledge *about* something gained by logic and thought, what we call "head knowledge." The other is knowledge by acquaintance, which is knowledge *of* something gained by our personal experience of it.

The knowledge of God that initiates and sustains relationship with Him is of both kinds. First, we know about Him by description. Knowing about Him then gives us a basis for acting upon and interacting with Him. He in turn acts upon us and interacts with us, the outcome being that we come to know Him by experience. Knowing Him by experience then enables and even quickens us to love, fear, trust, obey, and serve Him.

This sequential relationship between knowledge on the one hand and the elemental postures on the other thrust the answer to the question "Now what?" upon us. The first priority of disciples of Jesus is to know about the Father, the Holy Spirit, and Him by description. That head knowledge transforms into heart knowledge (by acquaintance) as we use it to act upon and interact with the living God.

The underlying assumption of this book is that we gain the head knowledge that enables heart knowledge by building a purposeful, objective, and thorough vision of Him. That assumption lies behind its aim, which is to assist you in doing just that. A.W. Tozer famously wrote that "What comes into our minds when we think about God is the most important thing about us."[53] I wholeheartedly agree. The truth is that our ideas about God are destiny determining to a degree that nothing else about us is.

I'd be remiss, therefore, if I didn't leave you with a parting word of challenge in light of it. Put first things first. Take the first step toward the abundance of life that knowing, loving, fearing, trusting, obeying, and serving God create and sustain. That first step is to see God clearly as He is. Build a vision of Him and make it 20/20!

APPENDIX

"IN A NUTSHELL"

God's Attributes Listed and Defined

#1 – Spiritual: He is non-material. He has no body and brain and doesn't miss them.

#2 – Self-existent: He has the power of being within Himself so that He has no cause or origin.

#3 – Eternal: He has always existed, exists now, and always will exist and is apart from time, not in it.

#4 – Triune: He is one being with three persons who form a community of indescribably magnificent personal beings of limitless goodness and greatness.

#5 – Omnipresent: Metaphorically, He is at the same time always present with His entire being in every place and in all space. Literally, every place and all space are "in" Him.

#6 – Omnipotent: He has limitless power so that He can do anything that can possibly be done.

#7 – Omniscient: He always knows literally everything that it's possible to know whether it's past, present, or future.

#8 – All-wise: He always knows what is best in every possible situation, always knows the best way to pursue what is best, and always pursues what is best in the best possible way.

#9 – Immutable: He is unchanging in His being. As He is now, He has always been and will always be.

#10 – Love: His affection for us, attention to us, and sacrificial action on our behalf are limitless and never ending.

#11 – Good: He is in His nature always disposed to do what is most beneficial and helpful to everyone and everything including Himself.

#12 – Gracious: He acts to give humans the good that they don't deserve. That good is physical and material provision to everyone, and forgiveness and perfection (increasing and finally full) to disciples of Jesus.

#13 – Holy: He always thinks, feels, and does what is morally good or right and never what is morally bad or wrong because He cannot, in His nature, do otherwise.

#14 – Wrathful: He always voluntarily reacts and responds adversely to sin.

#15 – Righteous: He always acts upon and interacts with everyone and everything according to His nature unaffected by anyone or anything outside of Him.

#16 – Just: He always does right by Himself and all moral beings (human and angelic) when He judges them.

#17 – Joyful: He possesses a permanent condition or state of beatitude with it accompanying emotional tones of happiness, hilarity, enthusiasm, passion, and delight.

FOOTNOTES

1. Dallan Forgaill. “Be Thou My Vision.” www.cyber-hymnal.org, n.d., accessed October 31, 2017.
2. Elton Trueblood (1960), *Foundations for Reconstruction* (Waco, Texas: Word Books), p. 12.
3. Jim Croce, “”You Don’t Mess Around with Jim”. Cashman and West, 1972.
4. Cornelius Platinga Jr., “Fashions and Folly: Sin and Character in the 90s,” (presented at the January Lecture Series, Calvin Theological Seminary, Grand Rapids, Michigan, January 15, 1993), pp. 14-15.
5. Bill Gaither. “You’re Something Special.” www.nametha-thymn.com, n.d., accessed October 2, 2017.
6. “Are God and the Devil Equal Opposites”. *Yahoo! Answers*, July 27, 2006. www.answers.yahoo.com/question/index.
7. A.W. Tozer (1961), *The Knowledge of the Holy* (New York, New York: HarperCollins Publishers Inc.), p. 2.
8. Dallas Willard (1997), *The Divine Conspiracy* (New York, NewYork: HarpersCollins Publishers Inc.), p. 389.
9. Robert Kunzig (2000, July 1), The Glue That Holds the World Together, *Discover* (online), www.discoverma-gazine.com/2000/jul/featgluons.
10. Tozer, *The Knowledge of the Holy*, pp. 29-30.

11. William Wilson (2001), *Alcoholics Anonymous*, 4th ed. (New York: Alcohol Anonymous World Services, Inc.), p. 62.
12. Wayne Grudem (1996), *Systematic Theology* (Grand Rapids, Michigan:Zondervan), p. 168.
13. C.S. Lewis (1962), *Mere Christianity* (London:Collins Clear-Type Press), pp. 137-138.
14. Willard, *The Divine Conspiracy*, p. 318.
15. Cornelius Platinga Jr. (2001), *Engaging God's World* (Grand Rapids, Michigan: Eerdmans), p. 20.
16. Hanover College. "Aristotle, Politics," www. history. hanover.edu/courses/excerpts/111aristotle.com, n.d., accessed July 23, 2017.
17. Shirl Hoffman (2010), *Good Game* (Waco, Texas: Baylor University Press), p. 146.
18. C.F. Keil and F. Delitzsch (1975), vol. VI of *Commentary on the Old Testament*, reprint (Grand Rapids, Michigan: Erdmans), pp.131-132.
19. Tozer, *The Knowledge of the Holy*, p. 74.
20. Blanchard Eades (1960), "If Jesus Came to Your House: And Other Poems," (Kansas City: Beacon Hill Press), p. 24.
21. Derek Kidner (1975), *Psalms 73-150: A Commentary on Books III-V of the Psalms*, (Leicester, England: Intervarsity Press), p. 333.
22. Bible Hub. "3841,pantofrator," www.biblehub.com/greek.htm, n.d., accessed August 23, 2017.
23. Willard, *The Divine Conspiracy*, p. 95.
24. Fred Belcher Jr., "Letters from a Modern Mystic." *Mere Christian Thoughts Blog*, September 16, 2017. www.merechristianthoughts.com, accessed September 27, 2017.
25. Anthony Campolo (1989), *Growing Up in America*, (Grand Rapids, Michigan: Zondervan), p. 187.
26. Ken Mandel, "10 Things People Forget Most Often." *Newsmax*, November 1, 2017. www.newsmax.com, accessed Novermber 15, 2017.

27. "Average Did You Knows." www.did-you-knows.com/did-you-know-facts/average.php?page=1, n.d., accessed August 4, 2017.
28. Erving Goffman (1959), *The Presentation of Self in Everyday Life* (Garden City: Doubleday Anchor Books), p. 173.
29. Willard, *The Divine Conspiracy*, p. XIV.
30. J.I. Packer (1973), *Knowing God*, (Downers Grove, Illinois: InterVarsity Press), p. 90.
31. Willard, *The Divine Conspiracy*, p. XIII
32. Felix Cavaliere and Eddie Brigati. "How Can I Be Sure." www.metrolyrics.com/how-can-i-be-sure-lyrics-younbg-rascals, n.d., accessed September 13, 2017.
33. Derek Kidner (1976), *A Time to Mourn, and a Time to Dance*, (Downers Grove, Illinois: InterVarsity Press), p. 38.
34. R. Alan Cole (1973), *Exodus: An Introduction and Commentary*, (Downers Grove, Illinois: InterVarsity Press), p. 228.
35. Leon Morris (1976), *The Epistles of Paul to the Thessalonians*, (Grand Rapids, Michigan: Wm. B. Eerdmans Publishing Compnay), p.34.
36. Brennan Manning (1994), *Abbas Child: the Cry of the Heart for Intimate Belonging*, (Colorado Springs, Colorado:NavPress), p. 47.
37. Thank You Notes. "Thank You Phrases – 40 Ways to Say Thank You," www.thank-you-notes.com/thank-you-phrases, n.d., accessed July 28, 2017.
38. Derek Kidner (1979), *Ezra and Nehemiah: An Introduction and Commentary*, (Downers Grove, Illinois: Intervarsity Press), p. 112.
39. Louis Berkhoff. *Systematic Theology,* www.monergism.com/thethreshhold/sdg/berkhof/systematic_theology, n.d., accessed October 14, 2017.
40. William Law (1955), *A Serious Call to a Devout and Holy Life*, (Louisville, Kentucky: Westminster John Knox Press), pp.21-22.

41. A.W. Pink. *Attributes of God*, www.chapellibrary.org, p. 36, n.d., accessed November 2, 2017.
42. C.S. Lewis (1970), *The Lion, the Witch and the Wardrobe*, (New York, New York: Macmillan Publishing Co,), pp. 75-76.
43. "Jesus Christ Was the Most Evil Man to Ever Live?" *Weknowtheanswer*, 2017. www.weknowtheanswer.com/q/jesus-christ-was-the-most-evil-man-to-ever-live, accessed September 9, 2017.
44. J.M. Barrie. *Peter Pan*, www.etc.usf.edu/lit2go/86/peter-pan/1559/chapter-8-the-mermaids-lagoon, n.d., accessed October 17, 2017.
45. C.S. Lewis. "The Weight of Glory." Sermon at the Church of St. Mary the Virgin at Oxford, England, June 8, 1942, www.issuu.com/the3nchanting/docs/the-weight-of-glory, accessed September 30, 2017.
46. "Teresa of Avila Quotes." *Goodreads*, www.goodreads.com/autor/quotes/74226.Teresa-of-vila, n.d., accessed October 28, 2017.
47. Joe Wittwer, "God Is Joyful." *Life Center*, December 24, 2015. www.lifecenter.net/sermons/2015/god-is-joyful.
48. G.K. Chesterton (1990), *Orthodoxy*, (Image Books: London, England), p. 60.
49. James Joyce, *A Portrait of the Artist as a Young Man*, (Planet eBook July 7, 2010, www.issuu.com/enciclopediapt/a-portrait-of-the-artist-as-a-young-man/198.
50. C.S. Lewis (1964), *Letters to Malcolm: Chiefly on Prayer*, (San Diego, California: Harvest), p. 93.
51. Dallas Willard (2002), *Renovation of the Heart*, (Colorado Springs, Colorado: NavPress), p. 133.
52. C.S. Lewis (1982), *The Screwtape Letters*, (New York, New York: Macmillan Publishing Company), p. 50.
53. Tozer, *The Knowledge of the Holy*, p. 1.

CPSIA information can be obtained
at www.ICGtesting.com
Printed in the USA
LVOW10s0140250518
578413LV00016B/184/P